SOUL FOOD

A SPIRITUAL GOURMET'S GUIDE TO PSALMS

By Rev. Dr. Validia M. Giddens

SOUL FOOD: A SPIRITUAL GOURMET'S GUIDE TO PSALMS

Copyright 2020 by Validia M. Giddens. All rights reserved. Independently published through Pokeberry Press, a division of Pokeberry Exchange, LLC., www. pokeberryexchange.com. No part of this book may be used or reproduced in any manner whatsoever without written permission except in the case of brief quotations embodied in critical reviews and articles. For information, Pokeberry Press, 41 N. Mercer St., New Castle, Pennsylvania 16101.

Books may be purchased for book club, educational, business, and promotional use. For information, email dr.validia.giddens@gmail.com with your request.

ISBN 9798687007849

FIRST EDITION

Printed in the United States of America

Book Design by Stephen V. Ramey

Cover background inspired by St. Mary's Church, Potton Bedfordshire UK

DEDICATION

To the women who raised me to love The Lord with all my heart, my mother, Gloria D. Roberts, my grandmother, Martha G. Swindler Pyles, and my great-grandmother Lena Jeter Jones

To my loving husband, Gregory S. Giddens and my son Theodore "Mitch" Mitchell for all their loving support and encouragement, I never could have completed this project without you.

Acknowledgements

To Almighty God who is the Alpha and the Omega, to Jesus Christ who is the Light of the World, and The Holy Spirit who reveals all truth, I am eternally grateful for the revelation of the Word of God and I am joyfully indebted as your life long servant.

To the men in the ministry who taught me to feast on the Word of God Rev. Burnett, Dr. Floyd Alexander, Dr. William R. Glaze, Dr. Charles O. Brown, Rev. McMahan Gray, and Dr. Laneer Fisher, thank you for all of your words of encouragement and unwavering support.

To those women who turned my dream into a reality, my sister Toni L. Jones, my friends A.J. Baughn and Michele Goodman- Jones, my "encouragers" and Krystin Murray Moore, my niece the editor.

My Prayer For The Readers Of This Book

Almighty God, allow this book to become a vehicle through which You manifest yourself in the life of the reader. May the Psalms become a source of daily sustenance to enrich their souls. May it also fill their hearts and minds with praise and worship unto You. Allow it to enhance their spiritual growth and bring a heighten sensitivity to the presence and work of the Holy Spirit as they feast on the Word of God. Amen and Bon Appetite

Contents

CHAPTER 1 1
    INTRODUCTION

CHAPTER 2 12
    THE APPETIZER

CHAPTER 3 18
    THE PALATE CLEANSER

CHAPTER 4 25
    THE MAIN COURSE

CHAPTER 5 47
    SIDE DISHES

CHAPTER 6 55
    OUR COMPLIMENTS TO THE CHEF

CHAPTER 7 65
    DESSERT

CHAPTER 8 72
    THE RIDE HOME

CONCLUSION 78

CHAPTER 1

INTRODUCTION

As Christians, we believe that when we accept Jesus Christ as our Lord and Savior we immediately receive the indwelling of the Holy Spirit. This initial interaction with The Holy Spirit has a profound effect on us. It can have the ability to transform us from our natural being who is under the influence of our human fleshly desires to the spirit filled being who possesses the capacity to succumb or submit to the will of God. The Holy Spirit, as the third person of the Trinity, is the spiritual presence which connects us to God. He is a person and as such He needs sustenance to survive. Just like the body requires food and nourishment to thrive, so must the soul be fed if it is to grow and flourish. Therefore we must give the Holy Spirit what He requires on a regular basis, the nutrients of the Word of God, which allows the affects and power of the Holy Spirit to become more evident in our lives.

To comprehend the indwelling and function of the Holy Spirit, we must first obtain a working knowledge of our human composition. Man is a triune being because he is created in the image of God. (Strauss, "2.

Man A Trinity (Spirit, Soul, Body) | Bible.org.", June 14, 2004)[1] According to the book of Genesis, *"God said, Let us make man in our image, after our likeness."* (Genesis 1:26, KJV).[2] We have been fashioned after our God, The Trinity. As a result, we are also trifold creatures in nature, comprised of mind, body and soul.

There has been extensive debate within the theological community about the threefold duplicity of man. There are those who believe that mankind is comprised of body, soul and spirit with the emphasis that the soul and the spirit are two different entities. According to the first book of the Thessalonians, *"And the very God of peace sanctify you wholly; and I pray God your whole spirit and soul and body be preserved blameless unto the coming of our Lord Jesus Christ"* (1 Thessalonians 5:23). Everyone appears to agree on the function of the body, which represents the physical structure that houses or contains the spirit and the soul. But the function and structure of the soul and spirit within man, for some, is still open to discussion. The bible does differentiate between the soul and spirit of man: *"For the word of God is quick, and powerful, and sharper than any two-edged sword, piercing even to the dividing asunder of soul and spirit, and of the joints and marrow, and is a discerner of the thoughts and intents of the heart"* (Hebrews 4:12). For the purpose of our examination of the book of Psalms we will agree with the following as cited in an article written by David J. Stewart "Understanding The Human Soul:"

> The soul is comprised of three elements: a mind to think, a heart to feel and a will to decide. Animals have a soul, but not a spirit. They do not have a spirit to fellowship with God, create music, write a poem or repent of sins. Animals cannot sin, nor do they comprehend sin. Animals act on behavioral impulse. Sometimes people

> behave like animals, but they do have spirits and know better, so they are held accountable by God. Man does not have a soul and spirit; but rather man is a soul and spirit. Man has a body. A person's spirit is their true being, their very existence, which is given by God alone. Ecclesiastes 12:7, "*Then shall the dust return to the earth as it was: and the spirit shall return unto God who gave it.*" As our creator, God gives the human spirit at conception, and our spirit returns into the Lord's hands the moment that we die. (Stewart, "Understanding The Human Soul.", December 1, 2012)[3]

Because man is both soul and spirit, we can ascertain that it is our soul and spirit, which are influenced by the presence of the Holy Spirit. Once the Holy Spirit establishes residency within the actual body, His impact is unmistakable. The scriptures convey a clear message to us about the many works of the Holy Spirit in the life of the believer: "*But the Comforter, which is the Holy Ghost, whom the Father will send in my name, he shall teach you all things, and bring all things to your remembrance, whatsoever I have said unto you*" (John 14:26). Watchman Lee states, in a collection of his works:

> Romans 8:16 says, "The Spirit Himself witnesses with our spirit" – not the heart or the soul – "that we are children of God." Man's spirit is the part where man works together with the Holy Spirit. How do we know that we have been saved and are the children of God? We know because our spirits have been made alive and the Holy Spirit lives in our spirit. Our spirit is a regenerated

and renewed spirit, and He who dwells in, yet is distinct from, our spirit is the Holy Spirit. He bears witness with our spirit within us.[4]

Therefore, within the context of our discussion, we will use the word spirit and soul interchangeably with respect to the regenerated soul of man, which is affected by the indwelling of the Holy Spirit.

The recognition of our sins and sinful nature allows us to identify the need for Jesus in our lives. So, we embrace Romans 10:9: "*That if thou shalt confess with thy mouth the Lord Jesus, and shalt believe in thine heart that God hath raised him from the dead, thou shalt be saved.*" It is through the realization of this biblical truth that we receive the gift of salvation. But acceptance of Christ as our risen Savior is only the initial step of our journey with The Lord. Salvation is an ongoing process. It takes a great deal of effort and a righteous attitude to establish and maintain a harmonious relationship with God. To facilitate this relationship, we must study the Word of God, communicate with Him, dwell in His presence and fellowship with those who share our beliefs.

This new found relationship creates a hunger and thirst for more of God in our lives: "*As the hart panteth after the water brooks, so panteth my soul after thee, O God*" (Psalms 42:1). We want to experience all God has to offer and move in the flow of the Holy Spirit. We want to be where God is and do those things that are pleasing in His sight. The soul within must be satisfied and so we begin to dine on the Word of God. The Holy Bible becomes a banquet table spread before us filled with a gourmet meal, an inevitable smorgasbord of spiritual delicacies. Initially, as we encounter the Word of God we may find ourselves drawn to the scriptures that relate best to our present circumstances and situations. Perhaps this is because God knows exactly what we need, and He meets us where we are. He invites us to receive His goodness and come into a special place of fellowship with Him. Like any good host, as the festivities begin, He is there to smooth any anxious wrinkles and infuse the occasion with the Spirit of hospitality and generosity. The chorus of this old gospel hymn may say it best:

> Come and Dine, The Master calleth, Come and Dine;
> You may feast at Jesus table all the time,
> He who fed the multitude, turned the water into wine,
> To the hungry calleth now, Come and Dine.[5]

Overview of the Book of Psalms

For this particular dining experience, The Lord has extended us an invitation to feast within the book of Psalms. The Psalms are one of the most beloved books of the Bible. The Psalms themselves are among the oldest poems in the world, and they still rank with any poetry in any culture, ancient or modern, from anywhere in the world. (Wright, The Case For The Psalms: Why They Are Essential, 2013)[6] The nature of the book is a collection of 150 sacred God inspired poems and songs, expressions of faith that were used publicly and privately as well as individually or corporately by the nation of Israel in times of prayer, praise, and worship. There are a variety of names ascribed to the book of Psalms:

The Hebrew title of this book is appropriately *Tehillim* ('praises'), for praise is a central feature of the poems that comprise this collection. The major Greek version rendered another Hebrew word, *mizmor* (song), found often in the titles of individual psalms, as *psalmos* (song), and they gave the book the title *Psalmoi* (songs). The common English title, of course, is 'The Psalms' and we can readily see its derivation from the Greek versions. Another popular English title, 'Psalter' comes from the Greek translation known as the Septuagint, which called the book *Psalterion*, meaning 'stringed instrument' (Bullock, Encountering The Book Of Psalms; A Literary and Theological Introduction, 2001)[7]

The Psalms are divided into five parts, reflecting the Pentateuch, or the first five books in the Bible. The first chapter of each section gives us a preface of what is to follow, while the last chapter is in the form of a doxology or a hymn of praise to God.[8] The divisions are as follows:

- Division 1 – Psalm 1 – 41 (41:13 doxology)
- Division 2 – Psalm 42 – 72 (72:19-20 doxology)
- Division 3 – Psalm 73 – 89 (89:52 doxology)
- Division 4 – Psalm 90 – 106 (106:48 doxology)
- Division 5 – Psalm 107 – 150 (150 the whole chapter doxology)[9]

The organizational structure of the Psalms is essential to its' interpretation because within each book there are themes that are stressed and others which are absent. Upon further examination of this construct we can ascertain a specific design intended to impact those who encountered the Psalms. Thus, the fivefold division is a deliberate editorial feature designed to emphasize the central place of the law (Torah) in Israel's faith.[10]

As a specific order of Hebrew prayers evolved within the Jewish faith many psalms were incorporated into the congregational prayer book.

> The practice of reading a daily psalm, which began with the Levites in the Temple, has become a standard

practice in the synagogue ritual in all Jewish communities. The reading of the psalm is preceded by the declaration: "Today is day [Sunday, Monday, etc.] on which the following psalm was recited in the Temple." According to custom, on the first day (Sunday), Psalm 24 is recited; on the second day, Psalm 48; the third day, Psalm 82; fourth day, Psalm 94; on the fifth day, Psalm 81; on the sixth day, Psalm 93; and on the seventh, and Sabbath day, Psalm 92.4. Many Jews today recite psalms daily, some completing the entire book each week; others completing it according to a monthly cycle.[11]

If we are to truly captivate the meaning of the Psalms we need to have a better understanding of elements of Hebrew poetry. The heart of Hebrew poetry is a style called parallelism, a literary pattern that states an obvious idea in one line and focuses more closely on the same idea in the following line, either repeating the thought in different terms or focusing on the thought more specifically.[12] Parallelism can be broken down into several subtypes, such as synonymous, antithetic and emblematic. Synonymous parallelism is the repetition of the same thought with equivalent expressions, the first line (or, stich) reinforcing the second and giving a distich (or, couplet).[13] Synonymous parallelism is the most common type found in the psalms. An example of this poetic style can be seen in Psalm 19:1-2:

The heavens declare the glory of God; and the firmament showeth His handiwork.

> *Day unto day uttereth speech, and night unto night showeth knowledge.*

Antithetic parallelism is a method of saying contrasting things in different lines and in different ways.[14] This literary feature can be seen in the book of Psalms as well as in Proverbs. Psalms 73:26 exemplifies this form of parallelism:

> *My flesh and my heart faileth: but God is the strength of my heart, and my portion forever.*

Emblematic parallelism is a third type, which involves a simile or a metaphor using imagery. The thought initially expressed in one line is compared to the thought in the next line. Psalm 42:1 presents an example:

> *As the hart panteth after the water brooks, so panteth my soul after thee, O God.*

Another type of parallelism is synthetic or progressive. Synthetic parallelism is the progressive flow of thought in which the second (or following) lines add something to the first, or explain it.[15] Psalm 1:3 is an excellent example:

> *Line 1: And he shall be like a tree planted by rivers of water*
> *Line 2: that bringeth forth his fruit in his season*
> *Line 3: his leaf also shall not wither*
> *Line 4: and whatsoever he doeth shall prosper*

The strophe, another element of Hebrew poetry found in the book of Psalms, is a logical unit determined by either the subject matter or the structure of the poem.[16] Psalms 19 is comprised of two strophes. The first six verses contain a hymn of creation and the last eight verses are a meditation on the law.[17] The strophe can take various forms such as an alphabet acrostic, which begins each new line or strophe with a letter of the Hebrew alphabet.

Another element of Hebrew poetry is the chiasm, derived from the Greek letter chi or (x). This devise may mark the structure of entire psalms or merely parts of psalms.[18] Psalm 8 demonstrates this structure. We begin with verse one given as a benediction, verses two and three attest to God's rule and verse four speaks of human meanness. The next verse, five refers to human greatness in direct contrast to the meanness mentioned in verse four. This becomes the central point where the ideas of the poem cross over. The psalm continues with verses six through eight speaking of humanity's rule and concluding with a benediction in verse nine.

As we continue our overview we must consider the literary genres contained in the psalms. There are numerous viewpoints on how the psalms should be categorized. Some feel that they should be grouped according to their function, others believe they should be classified by content, and many think they should be sorted by both. It is important to understand the genre of the Psalms simply because we do not read poetry in the same manner that we read prose or narratives. In addition, we must note that each genre has its own set of rules. First Chronicles 16:4 supports a three-tier classification approach, "to record, and to thank and praise the Lord God of Israel," which leads to three basic types – lament, thanksgiving and praise psalms.[19] Each basic classification can be further divided into seven literary genres contained in the book of Psalms. They are as follows:

1. Individual and communal lament psalms, or prayers for God's deliverance. These psalms speak to believers in moments of desperation and despair, when our need is for God's deliverance.
2. Thanksgiving psalms, consisting of praise to God for His gracious acts. These psalms make us aware of God's blessings and lead us to express our thanks with feelings of conviction.
3. Enthronement psalms, which describe God's sovereign rule. Through these psalms we acknowledge God as powerful Creator and sovereign Lord over all His creation.
4. Pilgrimage psalms, which were sung by worshippers as they traveled to Jerusalem to celebrate the Jewish festivals. These psalms can help us establish a mood of reverent worship.
5. Royal psalms, which portray the reign of the earthly king, as well as of the heavenly King of Israel. These psalms can make us aware of our daily need to make Christ the sovereign ruler of our lives.
6. Wisdom psalms, which instruct the worshiper in the way of wisdom and righteousness. These psalms are especially appropriate in times of decision when we are searching for God's will and direction in our lives.

7. Imprecatory psalms, in which the worshiper evokes God's wrath and judgment against his enemies. These psalms can help us be honest about our feelings towards people who have done us wrong and work our way through these feelings to a point of forgiveness.[20]

There is also a great deal of history included in the book of Psalms. The psalmists did not distinguish between history and theology the way modern people do today. Rather, they used poetry to convey history and history to convey theology; additionally, they used history to establish and prove qualities of God and His power and influence. When a historical person is mentioned in the psalms it is not necessarily for the person themselves but for the theological message or purpose behind that person.

This brief overview of the book of Psalms is intended to give the reader an ephemeral glimpse into its content and use for the children of Israel, as well as the modern-day believer. The Psalms are songs and poems that help us not just to understand this ancient and relevant worldview but also to actually inhabit and celebrate it.[21] Additionally, the Psalms can help us, obtain as well as maintain, a healthy well-nourished soul as we navigate the daily nuances of our Christian experience. The Psalms are the steady, sustained sub current of healthy Christian living.[22] So as we approach the banquet feast of The Lord we've taken a few moments to become acquainted with what's on the menu. Anyone whose heart is open to new dimensions of human experience, anyone who loves good writing, anyone who wants a window into the bright lights and dark corners of the human soul, anyone open to the beautiful expression of a larger vision of reality, and anyone who wants a close encounter with God should submerge themselves in the esoteric delight of these poems.

CHAPTER 2

THE APPETIZER

"Taste and see that the Lord is Good"

For most Christians we begin our journey with a simple confession of our faith. It may start at an altar call: "That if thou shalt confess with thy mouth the Lord Jesus, and shalt believe in thine heart that God hath raised him from the dead, thou shalt be saved" (Romans 10:9), or perhaps it took place at a street ministry where someone was handing out tracks and shouting "Jesus Saves." One thing is for sure: we all have a beginning in our faith, a place where we experience Jesus for the first time, a special time when we receive Him as our Lord and Savior so that He can establish residency in our lives. As we embark upon this Christian journey we find ourselves desiring more of Him; we hunger and thirst after righteousness because we want to know Jesus. We want to understand this new relationship with a God that loves us so much that He gave His only begotten Son so that we could receive forgiveness of our sins. And so with a simple confession of our belief in Jesus Christ we receive the indwelling of the Holy Spirit and the journey begins.

SOUL FOOD: A SPIRITUAL GOURMET'S GUIDE TO PSALMS

Often at this juncture, while we are still trying to figure it all out, someone who knows Jesus will point us to his or her favorite scripture verse or book in the Bible. They will encourage us to look to the Word of God to satisfy the longing of our soul for more of Him. For me, it was a hot summer afternoon listening to my Great Grandmother read the Thirty-Fourth Psalm. She had the habit of sitting on the porch and reading her Bible every Sunday after church. It had been about a month or two since that faithful day I walked down the aisle and received Jesus Christ as my Lord and Savior. It was at the tender age of eleven after a morning service filled with a preacher threatening hail and brimstone to the nonbelievers. But even after the joyful baptism celebration where I was to be transformed into a new creature in Christ, I still wanted and needed more. On that sunny summer day as I sat there with baited breath, "*I will bless the Lord at all times: his praise shall continually be in my mouth*" (Psalm 34:1), resounded across the front porch as if it were a statement of fact. "That sounds difficult," I thought to myself. Continual praise has to be impossible. As my Granny continued her recitation of the psalm, I contemplated the details of my salvation. "*O taste and see that the Lord is good*" (Psalm 34:8a), floated aimlessly through the air. "What do I have to do to 'taste' The Lord?" I wondered and at that moment there on the wings of the wind my senses were awakened and my appetite for the Word of God was roused.

An appetizer as defined by the D. K. Illustrated Oxford Dictionary is "a small amount to stimulate an appetite" (47) After we receive Jesus as our Savior, we become acutely aware that a portion of the Holy Spirit has been deposited within us. But we are just babes in Christ, and to reach maturity we must feed on the Word of God; "*As newborn babes desire the sincere milk of the word that ye may grow thereby*" (1 Peter 2:2) An appetizer entices our taste buds and brings us to a place of anticipation for the rest of the meal. The Psalms can serve as an appetizer into faith, and as we begin to delve into the Word of God, we find ourselves with a sense of expectancy for the course to follow.

Psalm Thirty-Four expresses a host of emotions experienced by a child of God who has just discovered the joy of Jesus: the excitement of being in the presence of the Most High God and never wanting the feeling to end. It's like falling in love for the first time and not wanting to be apart from the person who has now captured your heart. When God becomes the object of your passion, when He increasingly becomes the desire of your heart as you delight in Him, then you will discover joy indescribable (Bethany House, 2007).[23] David, the author of Psalms 34, knew such joy and he possessed a passion for the Lord that could not be contained.

David wrote this psalm after being forced to flee the country because of King Saul's rage. He went to the land of the Philistines to seek shelter. When he was caught and brought before Abimelech, he wanted to appear mad to escape persecution: he penned this psalm, and it worked. Interestingly, at a moment when David may have feared for his life, he was inspired to write a psalm that begins with praise for the Lord. Even in the face of adversity, David's love for God and his unwavering belief that He would delivery him from any situation was evident.

Psalms 34 can be split into two sections. Verses one through ten are in the form of a hymn, which offer praises to God. While the second half, verses eleven to twenty-two, become a sermon directly addressed to the listener, with verses fifteen through twenty-two consisting of a didactic teaching style. In addition, this is an alphabetical or acrostic psalm in Hebrew; each line of the poem began with a letter of the Hebrew alphabet in sequence from aleph to tau. It is impossible for us to capture this style in the English translation since there are twenty-two letters in the Hebrew alphabet and twenty-six in English, and a considerable number of Hebrew letters have no English correlate.

The following words resound with David's love for the Lord. A love that can be shared under any circumstance and without hesitation: "*I will bless the Lord at all times: his praise shall continually be in my mouth. My soul shall make her boast in the Lord: the humble shall hear thereof, and be glad*" (Psalm 34:1-2). David is resolved and fixed, *I will*; he is personally and for himself determined, let others so as they may; he is intelligent in head and inflamed in heart; he knows to whom the praise is due, and what is due, and for what and when.[24] This praise that David has for God silences his fears and elevates his faith to the point that it not only emanates from his soul but it also brings him excessive joy.

David continues with a testimony to God as the source of his salvation: "*This poor man cried, and the Lord heard him, and saved him out of his troubles*" (Psalm 34:6) When we look towards God, He will hear us and answer us and save us from all our troubles while squelching our fears. When we look to the world for a solution to our problems, we can be perplexed and lost, but looking to God allows us to have the supernatural peace bestowed by our heavenly father. And so, we sing a hymn of praise to our faithful unfailing God. We become deeply aware that God is all we need.

To discover the goodness of the Lord you must try it for yourself: "*O taste and see that the Lord is good: blessed is the man that trusteth in him*" (Psalm 34:8). Let us take a moment and review the three key elements of this verse, the words taste, see, and good. According to the Strong's Exhaustive Concordance the Hebrew word for taste is '*taam*'. It means to taste, see, or to discover by experience. The word see is translated '*raa*', which means to see, look, and view, to realize, to know, or to consider. While the word good is '*tob*' in Hebrew, meaning pleasing, desirable, and goodness. David is inviting the listener to discover by experience and come to know the goodness of God for himself. Charles Spurgeon in his expository of the Thirty-Fourth Psalm states:

> You can only know this really and personally by experience. There is the banquet with its oxen and fatlings; its fat things full of marrow, and wine on the lees well refined; but their sweetness will be all unknown to you except you make the blessings of grace your own, by a living, inward, vital participation in them.[25]

When you have seen God in action, you know that He truly blesses those who trust in Him and your faith is established. Faith is the soul's taste; they who test the Lord by their confidence always find him good, and they become themselves blessed.[26]

Like a good father, David is inspired to give instructions of what is expected of the children of God. "*Come, ye children, hearken unto me: I will teach you the fear of the Lord*" (Psalm 34:11). The word fear in this verse means reverence or piety. David is shifting the listener from a song of praise to a sermon on life. As children, when we begin to know God for ourselves, we must learn to approach Him with a sense of respect and humility. With wide eyed wonderment and a desire to do what is pleasing in His sight. Watching what we say, being responsible for our actions with the knowledge that the Lord is watching and listening inspirers the believer to abandon his life before Christ to fulfill his life with Christ.

David concludes the psalm with "The Lord redeemeth the soul of his servants: and none of them that trust in him shall be desolate" (Psalm

34:22). This statement of faith reminds us that through the precious blood of Jesus Christ we have been redeemed, delivered form sin and damnation. Because we have received Jesus as our Lord and Savior, we have been rescued from a life of desolation. We are now servants of the Lord and no longer slaves of this wicked and perverse world, bound by our sinful nature.

Psalms 34 embodies the deeply emotional experience shared by every new believer. When we come to that place where we are consumed, as David was, by a desire for more of God, we will find the passion and fullness of joy that can be experienced only in God's presence.[27]

CHAPTER 3

THE PALATE CLEANSER

As with any good gourmet meal we need to take a moment to cleanse our palate from the stimulating appetizer before we can dive into the main course. The cleansing of our taste buds gives us total appreciation for whatever the next course has to offer. This same process should be incorporated into our interaction with the book of Psalms. If we are going to properly digest the Word of God, we need to approach each encounter with the proper perspective.

The book of Psalms is comprised of a plethora of styles and genres. When you have a proper understanding of the original intent of each Psalm you can develop a better appreciation for what it brings to the table and essentially has to offer the soul. Now let us superimpose ourselves into these cherished hymns:

> The Psalms being hymns of praise, they only reveal their full meaning to those who use them in order to praise God. To understand the Psalms, we must experience the

> sentiments they express, in our own hearts. We must sing them to God and make our own all the meaning they contain. (Merton, Praying The Psalms, 1956)[28]

If we are truly ready to enrich our relationship with God and possess the depth of our relationship with Jesus Christ, we must begin to pray the Psalms. Gaining a personal application of the psalms will enable us to obtain the mind of Christ and purge us of anything and everything that would hinder our ability to hear from God and be in His presence. Our work in praying the Psalms is somehow to bring the stylized, disciplined speech of the Psalms together with the raw, ragged, mostly formless experience in our lives. (Brueggemann, Praying The Psalms: Engaging Scripture and the Life of the Spirit. Eugene, 2007)[29] How we partake of a meal at home or even our Grandmother's house can be quite different than when we go to a restaurant. So, it is with the Psalms. As formal and rote as they may be at church, when they are tailor made to fit our lives they become substantial.

> Scripture praying is using the Word of God as a means to communicate with the God of the Word. One of the great benefits of Scripture praying is that it helps us to express our thoughts, feelings and emotions to the Lord. One resource on praying Scripture puts it like this, "When we allow God's Word to be the vehicle of our prayers, it is capable of declaring deep inner desires and thoughts."[30]

As we incorporate the Psalms into our prayer life, we prepare ourselves for whatever God has in store. We know that with spiritual cleansing comes healing, deliverance, restoration and revelation. We want to position ourselves in a place where we not only experience God like the Children of Israel, but we also come to know Jesus as a personal friend. We want to become intimate with the Savior.

One aspect of praying the Psalms is to understand their Jewish origin. We know that when Jesus prayed He often quoted from the Psalms. As Jesus surrendered His life on the cross His final utterance is that of a Psalm: "*And at the ninth hour Jesus cried with a loud voice, saying Eloi, Eloi, lamasabachthani? Which is, being interpreted, My God, My God, Why hath thou forsaken me?*" (Mark 15:34). The outcry of Jesus is Psalm 22:1(a).

Jesus embraced His Jewish culture, customs and religion:

> For the prayers of Jesus are surly prayers of a Jew. He prayed as a Jew. And the entire tradition of the Christian prayer and Christian use of the Psalms must be seen in this light…the centrality of Jesus can never be seen far separated from the Jewish character of the material.[31]

What gives the psalms such a powerful impact is that they come from a place of sincere reverence for God and a longing to be in His presence. We find that the tremendous impact of the Psalms is buried at a very deep spiritual level, and that we must pray on that level in order to feel it at all.[32] They demonstrate a desire to please God while based on a foundation of trust in and for a God that is more than just the Creator but also the source of all provisions in life. That is the commonness of our faith as Christians and Jews; we come from the same place of confidence in God. We both desire a tangible relationship with our God. The Jewishness of the Psalms must be faced because our spirituality is diminished and trivialized if we neglect the Jewishness that belongs to our own tradition and practice of faith.[33]

Now that we have discussed the Psalms as Hebrew prayers that are rooted and grounded in the human experience we can begin to make them our own. When we pray the Psalms, we feed the soul. Pray the Word of God, as it is expressed in the Psalms, and these spiritual treasures will become our personal possession. You will discover the joy of walking in the Word, claiming its promise, and meditating upon its truths. (Richards, Praying the Psalms., 2003)[34] When we personalize the Psalms we begin to approach them with a sense of wide-eyed wonderment. We realize that not only are the Psalms words that were designed to speak to God, but also as the inspired Word of God, they are designed to speak to us from God. Praying the Palms enables us to see the duality of their content. Our individual commitment to praying the psalms says, "Lord I want to know you in the same manner as the psalmist. Father, I want to experience the intimacy of the Holy Spirit and the revelation of Jesus Christ." Faith is the key that unlocks the treasure chest known as the Book of Psalms, in which you will find a multitude of shining truths about God and His ways.[35]

A basic knowledge and understanding of the book of Psalms allows us to look at each psalm with an eclectic point of view. When I have a situation where I need the Lord to intercede on my behalf, I can choose a Lamentation Psalm as the impetus of my prayer. Or perhaps I may incorporate a psalm of praise or thanksgiving into my daily devotional to enhance my praise and worship time. I can use a Psalm of Degrees[36] to move me closer and closer into the presence of God. Or perhaps I want to recognize God for who He is in my life, so I choose a Kingly Psalm as the motivation for my prayer time. Familiarity with the contents of the book of Psalms enables us to peruse the banquet table of the Master with a discerning spirit.

Let us survey some examples of personalized psalms. "*The Lord is my Shepherd, I shall not want*", (Psalm 23:1) is a personal testimony by David to the Lord about their relationship. Consequently, the Twenty-Third Psalm is one that you may think has no need for further adaption. But let us turn this Psalm into a personal prayer:

> Lord God, you are my personal Shepherd. Because this is true, I know I shall never suffer want. Thank you, Father. It is you who makes me lie down in green pastures and it is you who restores my soul[37] (Psalm 23:1-3a)

Let us apply the concept of personalization to some additional Psalms:

> "I had fainted, unless I had believed to see the goodness of the Lord in the land of the living. Wait on the Lord: be of good courage, and he shall strengthen thine heart: wait I say, on the Lord" (Psalm 27:13-14)
>
> "Dear Father, I believe your Word, and I believe your goodness. Therefore, I wait on you in faith. Help me to be of good courage and strengthen my heart, as I wait on you. Thank you, father for hearing and answering my prayers. I believe in you with all my heart."[38]
>
> "Bless the Lord, O my soul, and forget not all his benefits: Who forgiveth all thine iniquities; who healeth all thy diseases; Who redeemeth thy life from destruction; who crowneth thee with lovingkindness and

tender mercies; Who satisfieth thy mouth with all good things; so that thy youth is renewed like the eagle's. (Psalm 103:2-5)

"O Lord God, my soul blesses you as I contemplate all your wonderful blessings in my life. Thank you, Father, for forgiving all my iniquities, healing all my diseases, redeeming my life from destruction, crowning me with your tender lovingkindness and mercy, satisfying my mouth with good things, and renewing my youth. Blessed by your name, Lord God."[39]

Notice in the examples given that you may choose to pray a portion of a particular psalm or one in its entirety. I would be remiss if I did not mention that there are those who believe the Psalms are designed to function as a complete set and that we should resist the tendency of picking and choosing based on necessity. N. T. Wright states the following:

> Things happen when you use the whole cycle (read five psalms a day, getting through them in a month) that are less likely to happen when you only use part or skip back and forth by following your own principle of selection rather than that of the compliers and we may suppose, the Holy Spirit. This, I think, is part of what it might mean to live as a community, or as an individual, under the authority of scripture."[40]

I believe the application of the Psalms to one's prayer life is a very individualistic endeavor. When we surrender our will to the power and authority of the Holy Spirit, He will guide us to a particular revelation of the use of the scriptures in every aspect of our lives. The Bible is a living word and as such it will speak to us in a very distinctive and personal manner. All we need is the ability to understand the meaning of the Psalms, their literal meaning as poems, and to "echo" or answer their meaning in our own experience; religious experience is born of loving faith.[41] By praying the Psalms as personal prayers from your heart, and applying them to your personal life and spiritual pilgrimage, you will see God, yourself and all your circumstances in an entirely new light.[42]

Our ability to go to God in prayer with a clean heart and a correct spirit is the key to digesting the Word of God, doing the will of the Father, and living a life pleasing to Him.

> The Psalms are filled with God's personal promises to you, His beloved child. As you speak to Him through these powerful passages, He will speak to you. Listen for His voice as you pray, waiting before Him in faith and expectancy.[43]

CHAPTER 4

THE MAIN COURSE

"The entrée featured for this evening will be…"

We have experienced the Book of Psalms as a spiritual appetizer as well as a palate cleanser for the soul. We will now examine what some consider three of the most popular psalms in the Bible. Each psalm brings its own individual appeal and flavor to the reader and can be referred to as spiritual staples or the main course of a healthy "Holy" diet.

Psalm 23 "Chicken"

Have you ever arrived at a wedding reception hungry? You survey the room looking for the banquet table ready to partake of the nuptial feast. An enticing array of aromas fills the room. The sweet smell of fruit and the mouth-watering scent of fresh baked bread tantalize your taste buds as they comingle in the air. You can't wait for the bride and groom to arrive so that the meal can begin. You take a sneak peek at the table, looking for your favorite dish and then you stop dead in your tracks. Your eyes roaming up and down the table frantically searching the table before you are faced with the stark reality: "There's no chicken and everybody loves chicken."

The Twenty-Third Psalm is the most well-known of all the psalms and is revered by Christians and Jews alike.[44] Like chicken, which is enjoyed universally by many, the Twenty-Third Psalm speaks to individuals of all faiths. These six simple verses have inspired believers for centuries and are an integral part of the worship services of those who have faith in the one True God.

Jewish traditions incorporate Psalm 23 in various manners. It is sung in Hebrew at the third Shabbat meal on Saturday afternoon.[45] It is also sung during the Yizkor (Remembrance) service,[46] a service in which prayers are recited by those who have lost one or both their parents. In contemporary Judaism these prayers may also be offered for any lost loved one. Sephardic and some Hassidic Jews also sing the twenty-third Psalm during Friday afternoon service and as part of the Sabbath night and day meal.[47] During Jewish holidays, it is read at the cemetery funeral service instead of the traditional prayer.

Within the Christian community, the twenty-third Psalm may be incorporated in a church service in a variety of ways. It can be utilized for an opening prayer or devotion as well as the springboard text of a Sunday morning sermon. It can provide the backdrop for Wednesday Night Prayer Meeting or be recited weekly at the end of Bible Study. The minister often quotes the entire psalm during a funeral processional and internment service. It may even be used daily as part of a personal devotional time. Whatever the case may be, it has become a mainstay for the followers of Jesus Christ. Walter Brueggemann writes the following:

> The function of this kind of psalm is theological, that is, to praise and thank God. But such a psalm also has a *social function* of importance. It is to articulate and maintain a "sacred canopy" under which the community of faith can live out its life with freedom from anxiety. ... There is a givenness to be relied on, guaranteed by none other than God.[48]

The Twenty-Third Psalm became especially popular when it was included in the Anglican Book of Common Prayers.[49] It is often associated with funerals and provides comfort for millions. The words: "*Yea, though I walk through the valley of the shadow of death, I will fear no evil.*" (Psalm 23:4a) have resulted in the association of this psalm with death and sadness. This verse has been quoted in popular culture in countless films and funeral scenes and even in Coolio's strangely poetic rap song, "Gangster Paradise."[50] The appeal of this verse can be seen throughout modern day society.

> The psalm has been set to music, to canvas, and to memory, frequently. But what continues to come as a surprise is the *range* of impact this psalm has. Psalm 23 is not just popular among the pious pew-sitters, to be found only in dusty old hymnals, or in the lyrics of the next generation of Christian songwriters. Psalm 23 is equally popular among the *popular*—in songs you might actually hear on the radio or movies that aren't released directly to DVD.[51]

There appears to be no limit to the influence of this psalm. Its appeal transcends religious and cultural lines.

> Psalm 23 is immensely popular and powerful for a wide variety of readers and prayers. It has been a powerful inspiration for art, a vibrant metaphor for theological imagination, and a critical component of personal reflection on the relationship of God with humanity. I am arguing that this is no less true for the references and appropriations of popular cultural—i.e., the secular or at least not explicitly "religious" references—than for the various applications of "religious" traditions. Indeed, they are perhaps all the more important because they are not burdened by issues of orthodoxy or faithfulness or even propriety.[52]

Traditionally this psalm is considered one of trust. David begins with "The Lord is My Shepherd," in present tense establishing a very personal relationship with the psalmist and God. The actual word David used in Psalm 23:1 is *Yahweh*, the proper and personal name of God as He made Himself known to the people of Israel. (Morgan, The Lord Is My Shepherd, 2013)[53] David the shepherd boy who became King, spent countless hours in the field tending the flock. Perhaps it was there that he came to know God personally.

> A songbird warbled cheerfully in the distance; the sheep chewed and bleated softly to one another in the foreground…long hours that rolled into weeks of careful attentiveness over his father's flocks; days of sitting and

pondering the nature of the universe and the God who created it, marveling at the intimate details of the grass beneath his feet and the utter magnitude of the sun and stars over his head. And somewhere in that stillness, with the edges of his heart, he sensed that the Creator of all of this, though greater than the universe itself, was always right there with him. A feeling so palpable that David wanted to reach out his hand and touch Him, but also so elusive that he knew simple, natural senses would never comprehend Him.[54]

Essentially, there are twenty-eight personal pronouns in these six verses, which constitute 25% of the entire text. No wonder William Evans, a writer of a hundred years ago, observed that the Twenty-Third Psalm is so universal because it is so individual.[55] As we come to know God as our personal Lord and Savior, like David, our minds begin to expand with the knowledge of His greatness and we are reminded of His immensity. It humbles our hearts, balances our thoughts, clarifies our perspectives, reassures our spirits and strengthens our souls, as we think rightly about God, everything else assumes proper proportions.[56]

The heart of this psalm is its graciousness. Not only are we reminded of all the loving caring qualities of *Yahweh* as the caregiver, but we also come to know Him as protector and provider. Even when we are faced with a seemly dead situation or problem that has no solutions, this psalm reminds us that we have no need to fear: He is there to comfort and keep us. The enemy may surround us on every side and there seems to be no way of escape, but God places before us a table filled with the proper provisions. Because God knows exactly what is required, the table may be a snack tray with just enough supplies for the moment, for His grace is sufficient enough, or a buffet where you can pick and choose what is needed in response to the situation over an extended time period. The table of the Lord is always available to His children. The Psalmist imagines God endowing him with material abundance; a set table, luxurious oil on the head, abundant drink.[57]

"*Thou anointest my head with oil; my cup runneth over*" (Psalm 23:5b). David includes anointing with oil at this point in the psalm, which is interesting for two reasons. First, as a shepherd, David knew that oil was often poured on the head of the sheep to make them slick so that lice and other insects did not get into the sheep's wool or ears. Oil was also rubbed into the sheep's little nicks and cuts to promote healing. These uses of oil would suggest that David was considering its healing properties. From this practice anointing became symbolic of blessing, protection and empowerment.[58] Secondly, we know that oil was used to anoint a person for a special office such as king or prophet. The New Testament Greek words for "anoint" are "*chrio*", which means, "to smear or rub oil" and, by implication, "to consecrate for office or religious service"; and *aleipho*, which means, "to anoint".[59] Therefore we can ascertain that David was also contemplating the spiritual significance of being appointed by God. When God places a calling on your life He will anoint you with the power you need to accomplish His will. It is the unction of the Holy Spirit. As seen in the first book of Samuel, "*Then Samuel took the horn of oil, and anointed him in the midst of his brethren: and the Spirit of the Lord came upon David from that day forward. So Samuel rose up and went to Ramah*" (1 Samuel 16:13). David experienced the influence of God's anointing.

Woven throughout the verses of the Twenty-Third Psalm is evidence of our Savior Jesus Christ as the Good Shepherd, the one who tends to our needs and watches over us as we navigate the ebb and flow of daily life: "I am the good shepherd: the good shepherd giveth his life for the sheep"... "I am the good shepherd, and know my sheep, and am known of mine" (John 10:11 & 14). In the Bible, "Christ" is a derivative of the Greek word Christos, meaning "anointed one" or "chosen one"; this is the Greek equivalent of the Hebrew word Mashiach or "Messiah".[60] Jesus is a transliteration of the Hebrew name Yeshua or Joshua, the Lord's human name given to Him by His mother Mary as instructed by the angel Gabriel. Christ is His title, not His surname, thus Jesus Christ means Yeshua (Yahweh is Salvation) the Mashiach or Joshua the Anointed One.

I had a Professor who concluded a class with a summary of the Twenty-Third Psalms, by comparing each line of the poem with a name given for God in the Old Testament. It reads as follows:

- The Lord is my shepherd – Jehovah Rohi (The Lord is my shepherd)
- I shall not want – Jehovah Jireh (The Lord will provide)
- He maketh me to lie down in green pastors: He leadeth me beside the still waters – Jehovah Shalom (The Lord is peace)
- He restoreth my soul – Jehovah Rapha (The Lord will heal)
- He leadeth me in the path of righteousness for his name sake – Jehovah Tsidqenu (The Lord is our righteousness)
- Yea, though I walk through the valley of the shadow of death, I will fear no evil – Jehovah Tsebaoth (The Lord of hosts)

- For thou art with me; thy rod and thy staff they comfort me – Jehovah Shammah (The Lord is there)
- Thou prepares a table before me in the presence of mine enemies – Jehovah Nissi (The Lord is conqueror or my banner)
- Thou anointest my head with oil; my cup runneth over – Jehovah Mekoddishkem (The Lord who sanctifies you)
- Surely goodness and mercy shall follow me all the days of my life – Jehovah Elyon (The Lord God Most High)
- I will dwell in the house of the Lord forever - El Olam (The Everlasting God or The Eternal God)

It is God's nature to be merciful, forgiving, and benevolent. He surrounds our lives with acts of grace we could never earn by our own efforts, all because of His loyal and steadfast love for us. Goodness represents all He bestows on us that we do not deserve. Mercy represents all He withholds that we do deserve.[61]

In a hundred words (only fifty-five in the original Hebrew), Psalms 23 sums up our needs in life and all the abundance of God's grace. It begins with "The Lord," and it ends with "forever." What could be better than that?[62]

Psalm 91 "Beef"

You're getting ready to return the R.S.V.P. card for the wedding reception. You check with your spouse to find out his or her preference. The options are Chicken Marsalis or a Delmonico steak. "I'll take the steak. I want something hearty and filling. Something I can sink my teeth in to because I don't want to be hungry when I get home after the wedding."

Psalms Ninety-One is not for those who are still on a spiritually soft diet. It is a psalm that takes the reader into the secret dwelling place of God to abide within His shadow. It is not a leisurely walk down a serene path; it is an expedition that requires commitment, faith and perseverance. (Potter, Psalms 91 The Dweller., 2009)[63] It requires a sense of spiritual fortitude and maturity of the believer. It is a journey for those who want to go to the next level in their relationship with God. It is a journey you must choose to take because it does not come automatically. It is a pilgrimage that benefits anyone and everyone who embark upon the endeavor. However, not all believers will desire, nor would they consciously choose, to begin such a journey.[64]

The first two verses of the Ninety-First Psalm give critical insight into God's character and establish the prerequisites for the dweller. *"He that dwelleth in the secret place of the Most High shall abide under the shadow of the Almighty. I will say of the LORD, He is my refuge and my fortress: in him will I trust".* (Psalm 91:1-2) The first verse of Psalm 91 incorporates two provisional elements, a condition and a promise. The condition, if you dwell in the secret place of the Most High there is the promise that you will abide in the shadow of the Almighty.

> The word rendered *dwells* in Psalm 91:1 means "to dwell, sit, abide, inhabit, remain." Dwells is a verb and shows action. It is something we do. A *shelter* is something that covers or affords protection. To "dwell in the shelter of" infers that there is a qualified need or purpose for some type of protection and that it must be available.[65]

As Christians, we should have a desire to come into the presence of the Lord daily. Abiding with God should come naturally, just like breathing. "The word "*abide*" means "to remain, lodge, or spend the night."[66] Our Christian journey ought to compel us to reside or spend extended time with God. "*So Jesus was saying to those Jews who had believed Him, 'If you abide in My word, then you are truly disciples of Mine; and you shall know the truth, and the truth shall make you free.'*"[67] Abiding or continuing in God's Word is a prerequisite for being free.[68] It allows us to be free from the worries and concerns of the world and rest in the comfort of Christ. It lets us experience God's love and the free gift of salvation. We must abide in God's Word so that we can grow in the knowledge of who God is and what He can do.

> There are countless well-meaning Christians who are content to be spoon-fed but are unwilling to tarry in the Word in order to glean its hidden treasures. They are not interested in lingering in the Scriptures long enough to mine the gems contained therein…They are unquestionably members of the kingdom of heaven but they will be content to forage in the shallows and remain

spiritually undernourished and will unnecessarily live below their potential.[69]

When facing certain challenging situations that require a spiritual safe haven we look to God to be our refuge and our fortress. A refuge is a shelter or a place of protection from danger.[70] A fortress is a fortified place where you can safely wage a counter measure against an enemy.[71] In times of distress and trouble God gives us the protection, direction and comfort we need. This shelter is simply a location that belongs to the Most High and He has given believers access to that shelter.[72]

There are four different names for God given within the first two verses of this psalm: Most High, Almighty, LORD, and God. Each name provides added insight into His character. The better we know the various meanings attached to God's name, the better we actually know Him.[73] We will take a brief look at each name within the context of Psalm 91.

I. Most High – The Hebrew word for Most High is "El Elyon." *El* means might or power and is also a reference to God Himself. *Elyon* reveals that God is the highest. He is the possessor of heaven and earth. The Most High is interested in delivering our enemies into our hand; He assures our victory and causes our enemies to experience certain defeat. If what we say and do lines up with truth from God who resides in our spirit, we will have met one of the criteria to dwell in the shelter of the Most High.[74]

II. Almighty – The Hebrew rendition of the word is "El Shaddai" and in most Bibles the word is translated as "God Almighty" or "Almighty God." *El Shaddai* means "most powerful in strength; omnipotent; He holds sway over all things. The ways of El Shaddai give us a clear picture of a God who is faithful to keep His covenants with His people. In order to abide in the shadow of the Almighty, we need to learn that El Shaddai is the One who nourishes, supplies, and satisfies. If we attempt to depend on our own resources we are not yet ready to abide in the shadow of the Almighty. The would-be dweller must first learn to dwell in the shelter of the Most High. Only then can he be prepared to abide in the shadow of the Almighty.[75]

III. LORD – The Hebrew word for LORD is "Yahweh" meaning "I Am." The English rendering of Yahweh is *Jehovah* and means "the active, self-existent One" and is written as LORD in most translations. You may have noticed that the word "LORD" is written in all capital letters. It is not to be confused with the Hebrew name for Adonai, which is written, "Lord" and has only the first letter of the word capitalized. We notice that the LORD is a stronghold for the oppressed and He does not forsake those who seek Him.[76]

> IV. God – *Elohim* is a plural Hebrew word usually written as *God* and means "the strong, faithful One; the only true God." It is Elohim who created the heavens and the earth and everything else that was brought into being. It was Elohim who created man in His own image. Elohim refers to and implies One who stands in a covenant relationship.[77]

The hopeful dweller declares, "I will say of the LORD" thereby making his intentions known.

> This is the starting point for the prospective dweller. A Christian cannot dwell before internalizing the declaration of this verse as his own. This verse identifies the dweller's commitment or vow, which God will not take lightly.[78]

The believer who makes this statement speaks from a place of experience where he has been in dire straits and witnessed the power of the Lord to overcome his enemies, or circumstances. He knows the ramifications of a covenant agreement and is not afraid to make a vow to the Lord. Webster defines a vow as a solemn promise or assertion, specifically one by which a person is bound by an act, service, or condition.[79] The psalmist knows this is a very solemn commitment and that God will expect the person who makes this kind of vow to take it seriously.

The words "I will say" compel us to move beyond the mere internal promise to a place of external commitment. Notice verse two begins with the words "I will say" and ends with "in him will I trust" because we must learn to verbalize our trust in the Lord. Trusting God is a choice. It does not come automatically. It is something that we learn over time with experience. There is a marked difference in knowing the promises of God and believing in them. As we begin to tell God how much we trust Him we gain more confidence in Him and a better understanding of His abilities.

God loves when we speak forth His Word. Literally, there is power in God's Word. The Bible tells us to do more than just meditate on the Word, but we must also speak the Word of God. Joel 3:10c says, "*Let the weak say, I am strong.*" Isaiah 55:11 says, "*So shall my word be that goeth forth out of my mouth: it shall not return unto me void, but it shall accomplish that which I please, and it shall prosper in the thing whereto I sent it.*" What we declare to God comes from a position of trust and obligation.

> So many times, as Christians, we mentally agree that the Lord is our refuge, but that is not good enough. Power is released in saying it out loud. When we say it and mean it, we are placing ourselves in His shelter. By voicing His lordship and His protection we open the door to the secret place.[80]

When we realize how important it is for us to place our faith and trust in God it gives us a sense of security. We learn to depend upon God as the source of not only our protection but also all our needs.

> Simply because a Christian verbalizes verse two to the LORD does not make that verse experientially true. Who

> then can scripturally speak Psalm 91:2 to the LORD? He who dwells in the shelter of the Most High can confidently declare that the LORD is his refuge and fortress. He who dwells in the shelter of the Most High can trust in his God because of what he has learned.[81]

We have learned to trust God and we know Him as our deliverer and immediate protector like a shield keeping us out of harm's way. Because He is our protector, we are no longer fearful of the emanate danger that surrounds us. We know that God has the power to defeat a thousand on one side and ten thousand on the other. He has dispatched Angels to watch over us. This trust we have in God is reassurance that during everyday life with evil lurking on every corner, we are under God's umbrella of protection.

> There is a uniqueness about this psalm. Promises of protection can be found throughout the Bible, but Psalm 91 is the only place in the Word where all the promises are brought together in one collection, forming a covenant written through the Holy Spirit.[82]

The final three verses of Psalm Ninety-One move us from the prospective of the psalmist to the view point of God. In Psalm 91:14 we have arrived at the point where God speaks:

> There are two voices speaking in the earlier part of this psalm: one that of a saint who professes his reliance upon the Lord, his Fortress; and another which answers the former speaker, and declares that he shall be preserved by God. In this verse, which is the first of the final portion

of the psalm, we have a third voice-the voice of God Himself, which comes in to seal and confirm, to heighten and transcend, all the promises that have been made in His name.[83]

Throughout the Ninety-First Psalm, the voice of the season dweller has been speaking to the potential dweller about the benefits of being in the shelter of the Most High God. Now it is God's turn to affirm what has been stated with guarantees. He begins with a conditional statement "Because he has set his love upon me, therefore will I..." (Psalm 91:14a). God clarifies that as a result of the reciprocating love between Him and the psalmist He will do all that has been promised and even more.

> The word for love in Deuteronomy 7:7 is the same word used in Psalm 91:14, *chashaq*. Strong's defines the word as meaning, "to *cling*, that is, *join* (figuratively) to *love*, *delight* in, (have a) desire." When the Lord *set his love*, He chose to love the unlovely and the unworthy in Deuteronomy 7:7...By using the Hebrew word *chashaq*, the Scripture is saying that the dweller clings to, joins, and truly delights in his God.[84]

The Lord spends the concluding verses of the psalm proclaiming what He will do for those that love Him. He will deliver them and set them on high. He will answer them when they call and be with them in the time of trouble. And He will guarantee them a satisfying life for as long as they live and grant them salvation, which is everlasting life. It seems quite fitting that the final word of this psalm points to Jesus. The Old Testament proposes the coming Messiah while the New Testament reveals

His manifestation. Every time salvation is mentioned in the Old Testament it directs us to Jesus the Christ. The person of the Godhead who came to earth to justify our relationship with God.

> *"For God so loved the world, that he gave his only begotten Son, that whosoever believeth in him should not perish, but have eternal life.*
> *For God sent not his Son into the world to condemn the world; but that the world through him might be saved."*
> *(John 3:16-17)*

Psalm 150 "Fish"

Most people consider fish to be a light fare, a dish that is satisfying but not filling. It is an entrée that has a very distinct texture and taste to the discerning palate and is loved by some and despised by others. It can be prepared in a variety of ways: fried, baked, broiled or poached, just to name a few. While some cultures incorporate it as a staple in their diet, there are those that find it offensive or even an insult to serve. In other words, it is not for everyone but if you enjoy it you probably can't get enough of it.

The final entry in the book of Psalms is a song of praise. Psalm 150 discusses various attributes of offering praise to God. The Bible tells us that praise is pleasing to God and encourages us to include it as part of our communication with Him: "*Through Him then, let us continually offer up a sacrifice of praise to God, that is, the fruit of our lips that give thanks to His name. And do not neglect doing good and sharing; for with such sacrifices God is pleased*'. (Hebrews 13: 15-16)[85] Consequently, there are congregations where offering praises to the Lord are an essential aspect of the worship service and their daily prayer life. The congregation will erupt into praise with the mere mention of the name of Jesus accompanied by dancing, singing and shouting without any prompting. This is considered an outpouring of the Holy Spirit and the believer's willingness to surrender His will. Others may incorporate this request into their interaction with God in a different manner. There are those who believe praising God is intrinsic and personal. Their praise may consist of singing a hymn, clapping or waving their hands or just experiencing quiet moments of retrospection from their hearts.

As we take a closer look at Psalm 150, let us examine its content and take note of what it tells us about praise. Simply stated, God should be praised:

- The Where of Praise (verse 1) – God's sanctuary refers to the place of worship on earth where God's people gathered. In the psalmist's day, this was the temple in Jerusalem; in ours, it is the church. The "mighty expanse" ("firmament") refers to the heavens and is a call to all of the heavenly hosts to praise God. Thus, the psalmist is saying, "Praise God everywhere! Praise Him on the earth! Praise Him in the heavens!"[86] God enjoys the praises of His people.
- In His personal Holiness
- In the person of His Son
- In heaven
- In the assembly of the saints
- In the silence of the heart

- The Why of Praise (verse 2) - Why should we praise God? Because of what He has done ("His mighty deeds") and because of who He is ("His excellent greatness").[87] As you reflect on God's Word we should be reminded of the great things He has done. He knew us before we were formed in our mother's womb. He will satisfy us with long life. He sent us salvation through His Son Jesus the Christ.
- Apart from His many mighty deeds, God is worthy of praise simply for who He is. He is perfect, lacking in nothing.[88] Our God is the Only God. He is the God who made heaven and earth. He is the King of Kings and Lord of Lords. There is no other like Him in all the earth. He is omnipotent, omnipresent and omniscience. He is a sovereign God. He is worthy of all the praise.
- The How of Praise (verse 3-5) - The sense of these verses is, "Pull out the stops and give it everything you've got!" Use your breath to blow the trumpet; use your fingers to play the harp and lyre; use your whole hand to hit the tambourine (timbrel); move your whole body in the dance. There are stringed instruments, wind instruments, and percussion instruments (vv. 4-5) ...we ought to come with the fervency and expectancy as if Jesus Himself

were going to be present, because He is here. He deserves our giving Him everything we've got in worship.[89]

- The Who of Praise (verse 6) - The only qualification for praising God is that you breathe. [90] This statement would include everything that is living on this earth. From the largest Redwood to the smallest amoeba, every plant and animal exhibits some aspect of breathing to sustain life. Thus, they are commanded to praise God with their very existence. The fact that God can command us to praise Him means that praise is not just a feeling based upon your mood or circumstances.
- Praise is in part a feeling, but it is not at its heart a feeling. Praise is a matter of obedience to our great God. It stems from deliberately focusing on Him. It is the result of being willfully God-centered in your thinking. If you are breathing, praising God is not an option; it is your responsibility.[91]

When we consider the importance of praise, with respect to God, we should be mindful of the benefits of praise. Praise can maintain or restore our relationship with God. Praising God improves our outlook on life and our attitude about daily circumstance. It reminds us that God is in control of everything and praise keeps our focus on Him.

SOUL FOOD: A SPIRITUAL GOURMET'S GUIDE TO PSALMS

God taught the Israelites the importance of praise. Within the Hebrew language there are numerous words associated with various forms of praise. We will take a moment to look at seven Hebrew words commonly used in the Bible to reference praise:

1. Halal - Halal is a primary Hebrew root word for praise. Our word "hallelujah" comes from this base word. It means "to be clear, to shine, to boast, show, to rave, celebrate, to be clamorously foolish." (Psalm 149:3 & Psalm 150:1)
2. Yadah - Yadah is a verb with a root meaning "the extended hand, to throw out the hand, therefore to worship with extended hand." According to the Lexicon, the opposite meaning is "to bemoan, the wringing of the hands." (Psalm 63:1 & Psalm 107:15)
3. Towdah comes from the same principle root word as yadah, but is used more specifically. Towdah literally means "an extension of the hand in adoration, avowal, or acceptance." By way of application, it is apparent in the Psalms and elsewhere that it is used for thanking God for "things not yet received" as well as things already at hand. (Psalm 50:14, 23)
4. Shabach - Shabach means "to shout, to address in a loud tone, to command, to triumph." (Psalm 47:1 & Psalm 145:4)

5. Barak - Barak means "to kneel down, to bless God as an act of adoration." (Psalm 34:1 & Psalm 95:6)
6. Zamar - Zamar means "to pluck the strings of an instrument, to sing, to praise; a musical word which is largely involved with joyful expressions of music with musical instruments. (Psalm 66:2-4 & Psalm 149:3)
7. Tehillah - Tehillah is derived from the word halal and means "the singing of halals, to sing or to laud; perceived to involve music, especially singing; hymns of the Spirit. (Psalm 22:3 & Psalm 33:1)[92]

Praising God allows us to express our feelings to and about the Creator. It brings us into the presence of God with the proper attitude of reverence, respect and thanksgiving. It draws us nearer to Jesus, as we demonstrate our love for our personal Lord and Savior. And Praise allows us to share our love with God and receive His never-ending unconditional love in exchange.

CHAPTER 5

SIDE DISHES

When we have the opportunity to sit down to a gourmet meal we usually do so with certain expectations. Most meals consist of four courses comprised of the following components:

- First Course is a hot soup or raw fish used to stimulate the appetite.
- Second Course is a combination course of cooked food such as meat, starch, vegetables, and a garnish.
- Third Course is usually a crisp toss salad with a tart dressing.
- Fourth Course is the sweet dessert, which follows.[93]

The meat is considered the main course and the starch and vegetables are the side dishes, the food that accompanies the meat to make a complete meal.

In this section we will take a brief look at a few of the verses in the book of Psalms that are used to minister to individuals outside of the context of their entire psalm. Perhaps these scriptures have become near and dear to our heart because of their frequency. Maybe God has written them on the fleshy tables of our heart because they speak volumes to the human experience. Nevertheless, these are those snippets of Psalms that our spirits cling or gravitate to even though we may not know where to find them. They have become our spiritual side dishes.

They are listed below randomly as the Lord put them upon my heart:

Guidance

- Thy word is a light unto my feet, and a lamp unto my path. (Psalm 119:105)

Desires

- Delight thyself also in the Lord; and he shall give thee the desires of thine heart. (Psalm 37:4)

Provision

- I have been young, and now old; yet have I not seen the righteous forsaken, nor his seed begging bread. (Psalm 37: 25)

Safety

- I will lift up mine eyes unto the hills, from whence cometh my help. My help cometh from the Lord, which made heaven and earth. (Psalm 121:1-2)

Wisdom

- Let the words of my mouth, and the meditation of my heart, be acceptable in thy sight, O Lord, my strength, and my redeemer. (Psalm 19:14)

Trust

- The Lord is my light and my salvation; whom shall I fear? The Lord is the strength of my life; of whom shall I be afraid. (Psalm 27:1)

Creation

- The earth is the LORD'S and the fullness thereof; the world, and they *hat dwell therein.* (Psalm 24:1)

Faith

- I had fainted, unless I had believed to see the goodness of the LORD in the land of the living. (Psalm 27:13)

Wisdom

- The steps of a Good man are ordered by the LORD: and he delighteth in his way. (Psalm 37:23)
- Behold, how good and how pleasant it is for brethren to dwell together in unity! (Psalm 133:1)

Praise

- Bless the LORD, O my soul: and all that is within me, bless his holy name. (Psalm 103:1)
- LORD our Lord, how excellent is thy name in all the earth! (Psalm 8:9)

This is a brief list of some of the most memorable scriptures found in the book of Psalms. It is a mere reflection of their impact and how easily they flow from our spirit. These verses are so common they are memorialized in song, and masterfully used by worship leaders to encourage the congregation to new heights. They echo from pulpits and prayer circles everywhere because in them you can hear the resounding voice of the Lord. These verses have become our side dishes: portions of scripture that complement our Christian experience and fill our souls with reassurance and hope. Before we even knew they were psalms they resonated in our spirits because they ministered to our souls. Perhaps they resonate because they emerge from the heart of the psalmist who knows where God dwells, or because they reflect the trials and triumphs of humanity. The Psalms were written in the psalmist greatest hour of desperation or their highest elation of joy.

The psalms are poetry set to music that transform both the singer and the listener. It is this profound impact, which makes even the smallest stanza unforgettable. The psalms speak of change, but more importantly they are agents of change: change within the humans who sing them, and change through those humans, as their transformed lives bring God's kindness and justice into the world.[94] When we accept Jesus as our Lord and Savior we become the vehicles through which the Kingdom of God is established here on earth. The unexplainable change that others see in us, which point to Jesus as the true Messiah. As New Testament Christians we can allow the psalms to minister to us and then through us the nonbeliever will see the manifestation of Christ in our lives.

Let us look at a few of the Bible verses that encourage us to partake of the Word of God for spiritual nutrition. Psalm 143:6 reminds us of the thirst of the spirit: "*I stretch forth my hands unto thee: my soul thirsteth after thee, as a thirsty land.*" During the Sermon on the Mount, Jesus speaks of spiritual fullness for those who seek it, "*Blessed are they which do hunger and thirst after righteousness: for they shall be filled*" (Matthew 5:6). Within the confines of The New Testament, Jesus refers to Himself as both bread and water:

- I am the bread of life: he that cometh to me shall never hunger; and he that believeth on me shall never thirst. (John 6:35)
- Jesus answered and said unto her, Whosoever drinketh of this water shall thirst again: But whosoever drinketh of the water that I shall give him shall never thirst; but the water that I shall give him shall be in him a well of water springing up into everlasting life. (John 4:13-14)
- In the last day, that great day of the feast, Jesus stood and cried, saying, if any man thirst, let him come unto me, and drink. He that believeth on me, as the scripture hath said, out of his belly shall flow rivers of living water. (John 7: 37-38)

We know that Jesus was not speaking to our physical bodies. He was not suggesting that we literally eat or drink Him but was appealing to our immortal souls. He prompts us to feed our spirit with His word and dwell in His presence so that we can be filled with the power of the Holy Spirit. Then we will not have to rely on our own thoughts or judgment to determine our path in life. We merely must surrender our will and follow the directives of our God who is "*a lamp unto my feet and a light unto my path*". (Psalm 119:105)

In the book of St. John, Jesus speaks figuratively in a parable to the Jews about consuming his flesh:

> "*I am the bread of life. Your fathers did eat manna in the wilderness, and are dead. This is the bread which cometh down from heaven, that a man may eat thereof, and not*

die. I am the living bread which came down from heaven: if any man eat of this bread, he shall live forever: and the bread that I will give is my flesh, which I will give for the life of the world." (John 6:48-51)

As Jesus refers to Himself as the sustainer of life, both bread and water, we are reminded of the migration of the Children of Israel from Egypt. The Israelites spent forty years in the desert as they attempted to travel from Egypt to Canaan. During this time God gave them whatever provisions were necessary to sustain life. When they found themselves without water He gave Moses instructions to bring forth water from a rock: *"And the LORD said unto Moses, Go on before the people, and take with thee the elders of Israel; and thy rod, wherewith thou smotest the river, take in thine hand, and go. Behold, I will stand before thee there upon the rock in Horeb; and thou shalt smite the rock, and there shall come water out of it, that the people may drink. And Moses did so in the sight of the elders of Israel"* (Exodus 17:5-6). As Moses strikes the rock we are reminded of our Living Water, Jesus, who is both our rock and salvation. When hunger caused the children of Israel to complain in the Wilderness, God sent them substance in the form of manna: *"Then said the LORD unto Moses, Behold, I will rain bread from heaven for you; and the people shall go out and gather a certain rate every day, that I may prove them, whether they will walk in my law, or no…And when the children of Israel saw it, they said one to another. It is manna: for they wist not what it was. And Moses said unto them, This is the bread which the LORD hath given you to eat."* (Exodus 16:4 & 15) Jesus is the Bread of Life sent down from heaven to give eternal life to everyone who receives Him.

It is not a surprise that the Forty-Second Psalm begins the second division of this beloved book: "As the hart panteth after the water brooks, so panteth my soul after thee, O God. My soul thirsteth for God, for the living God: when shall I come and appear before God?" The second division of the book of Psalm, which correlates to the book of Exodus in the Torah, addresses thirsting for God in the time of trouble. The image of a thirsty deer invokes an image of our own insatiable thirst:

> Yet it is only an image that bespeaks a deeper thirst we all have but, alas, are not always in touch with or do not identify. It is the deep thirst that we have, rising from the very depths of our being; as Saint Augustine wrote, "Our hearts are made for you, O Lord, and they will not rest until they rest in you." (Pennington, Psalms: A Spiritual Commentary, 2008)[95]

How appropriate for the psalmist to use a deer literally crying out for water to draw upon our imagination. Joel 1:20, makes a reference to the beast in the field which cry out because the river waters have dried up.

> The word "cry" used here is the same Hebrew word used in Psalm 42:1 for "panteth." These animals were groaning and crying out from the very depth of their being for water. The groans and cries did not come from their head or their heart but from deep within. What a powerful picture used by David to depict the longing in his soul for God.[96]

Thanks be to God for the longing within our hearts that draws us nearer to Him each day.

CHAPTER 6

OUR COMPLIMENTS TO THE CHEF

Authors of the Psalms

World-renowned chefs are admired for their knowledge and ability. They take the simplest ingredients and put them together to create a unique blend of flavors. They are familiar with the combination of elements required to produce the perfect dish and know how to delight the palate. No need to measure anything: a pinch of this and a dash of that and voila, you have your gourmet meal.

The authors of the Psalms were more than mere poets they were master chefs. They were artists who had the ability to evoke emotions, drawing pictures in the minds of individuals and invite the presence of God into their midst. The psalmists voiced their adoration for the God of Israel, for the Psalms are the songs of men who knew who God was.[97] Words were at their command, strung together effortlessly creating melodious hymns as they stretched forth their hands to the Lord. The authors of these psalms reflect the cavalcade of individuals who yearned to communicate with God.

It is clear that one hundred and fifty psalms were written by many different people across a period of a thousand years in Israel's history.[98] These poems and songs contain not only the history of the nation of Israel but the individual stories of those who penned them. The Psalms name more than seven authors, including five individuals and two families.

Here is a list of those who contributed to their content:

- **David**: The God-anointed king of Israel. (1 Samuel & 2 Samuel)
- **Asaph (the family)**: Asaph and his sons were ordained by David to lead the people in worship and were recommissioned when Nehemiah rebuilt Jerusalem. (1Chronicles 25:1; Nehemiah 7:44; 12:46-47).
- **The sons of Korah (another family)**: in the book of Numbers, a man named Korah rebelled against Moses and Aaron. God caused the earth to swallow him up. His sons survived, though (Numbers 26:11), and continued to serve in the house of the Lord. They share one psalm (Psalm 88) with the wise man Heman.
- **Heman**: He was a wise man who co-authored the eighty-eighth psalm with the sons of Korah. His brother Ethan (1 Chronicles 2:6) wrote a psalm, too.
- **Solomon**: The king who is better known for his work in Proverbs, Ecclesiastes, and Song of

Solomon. He's David's son, and inherits his father's throne.

- **Moses**: He wrote more words in the Bible than any other human. Most of those words are in the books of Genesis, Exodus, Leviticus, Numbers, and Deuteronomy. Moses also wrote a psalm.
- **Ethan the Ezrahite**: We do not know much about him except that he was a famous wise man. His wisdom was so well known, in fact, the Bible makes a point to tell us that Solomon was wiser. (1 King 4:31).[99]

Theologians appear to agree on who wrote the psalms but there seems to be some discrepancy on exactly how many psalms were written by each of the authors. This summary of the authors provided by Charles R. Swindoll in his Bible teaching on the book of Psalms constitutes one assessment:

> Some psalms name their author in the first line. For example, Moses wrote Psalm 90. David was responsible for many of them, composing seventy-three psalms. Asaph wrote twelve; the descendants of Korah penned ten. Solomon wrote one or two, and Ethan and Heman the Ezrahites were responsible for two others. The remainder of the psalms do not contain information about their authors.[100]

Jack Zavada in his article on the Book of Psalms gives the following estimate:

> David 73, Asaph, 12; Sons of Korah, 9; Solomon 2; Heman1; Ethan 1; Moses 1; and 51 anonymous.[101]

Here is a breakdown of the psalms written by people other than David:

- The family of Asaph wrote 12 psalms:
    - Psalm 50
    - Psalms 73–83
- The sons of Korah wrote 11 psalms:
    - Psalm 42
    - Psalms 44–49
    - Psalms 84–85
    - Psalms 87-88
- Heman the Ezrahite coauthored Psalm 88 with the sons of Korah.
- Solomon wrote two psalms:
    - Psalm 72
    - Psalm 127
- Moses wrote Psalm 90.
- Ethan the Ezrahite wrote Psalm 89.[102]

You will notice the discrepancy between the number of psalms attributed to the sons of Korah in the aforementioned articles and the chart provided by Jeffrey Kranz. The numerical difference reflects the discrepancy mentioned previously in this chapter. Identifying Old Testament authorship can be difficult. In the book of Psalms, the subscript below the title denotes the author. Therefore, psalms that do not list a specific author may be assigned one base on content and speculations. For example, there are those who believe Psalm 91 was written by Moses after the dilemmas he faced in the wilderness based on its content, style, and the fact that if follows Psalm 90.

Apart from Moses, Solomon, and David himself, the other authors were priests or Levites who were responsible for providing music for the sanctuary worship during David's reign. We will now take a glimpse into the life of two of these psalmists.

David is the most well-known author of the psalms. He is credited with seventy-three of the entries. One Talmudic source and nearly all the orthodox Jews believe that King David was the author of all the psalms, for he is known in the Bible as "the hero of Israel's Songs" (2 Samuel 23:1).[103] David's life as a shepherd, a psalmist, a warrior, a fugitive and a king can be outlined in the content of his lyrics. The poetic talent of David, his personal influence, and the landscape of his life are revealed throughout the psalms.[104]

Here are a few examples:

- Psalm 59, when Saul sent men to watch David's house and kill him (1 Samuel 19:11)
- Psalm 56, when David fled to Gath (1 Samuel)
- Psalm 34, when David pretended to be insane (1 Samuel 21:13)
- Psalm 142, when David escaped to the cave of Adullam (1 Samuel 22:1)
- Psalm 52, when Doeg the Edomite informed Saul where David was located (1 Samuel 22:9)

- Psalm 54, when the Ziphites betrayed David to Saul (1 Samuel 23:19)
- Psalm 57, when David was hiding from Saul in a cave (1 Samuel 24:1)
- Psalm 18, when David spared Saul (1 Samuel 24:11–12)
- Psalm 32, when David received forgiveness for his sin with Bathsheba (2 Samuel 12:13–14)
- Psalm 51, when David confessed his lustful and deceitful sin with Bathsheba (2 Samuel 12:13–14)
- Psalm 3, when David fled from Absalom (2 Samuel 15:14–16)
- Psalm 63, when Ziba refreshed David and his men (2 Samuel 16:2).[105]

David, the shepherd boy who would be king, had the perfect atmosphere to become a psalmist. He spent endless hours tending his father's herds in grassy fields by the steam. Within the sound of the babbling brook he detected the voice of Adonai. While he watched the panorama of clouds floating across the sky, leaning against a nearby olive tree, he could sense Elohim. David saw the handiwork of God within the beauty of nature. He perceived God's existence and so even as a young boy he began to sing songs of praise and thanksgiving to the Creator.

Unbeknownst to David, God had a plan for his life, one that would move him from obscurity to prominence as the beloved king of Israel. There would be many moments of pain and glory along the way but for each step of the journey God put a song in David's heart. So, when King Saul calls for David to come and play music to calm his nerves, Jesse

David's father could not refuse but wondered what was in store for his son next.

> It had been a strange event. Though Samuel had made a great fuss about calling David, once David arrived and Samuel anointed him, Samuel said nothing more about it…It was as if all he had ever intended to do was anoint David in a quiet ceremony and then get out of town before too many notice he was there. Jesse notice that since Samuel's coming David had changed. Favor seemed to follow him.[106]

David was both excited and unnerved as he went to the palace to play for the king. David knew that Saul had been chosen by God to lead Israel, and David believed it to be a great calling that deserved his deepest respect and devotion.[107] As he ministered to the king in the place, lyre in hand, a chain of events was set into motion that would shape the course of David's life.

David's musical genius and commitment to the worship of God cast a refreshing shadow over the entire book of psalms.[108] David poured out his life into his music. As you read the psalms written by David, you become acutely aware of his circumstance and you sense his desire to commune with God in every situation.

David lived an adventurous life filled with extreme ups and downs. David was Israel's greatest and truly ideal king. He was a great warrior and a man who loved God. He brought great peace and prosperity to the land.[109] But David was a man filled with human frailty and wickedness. He committed adultery and was a murderer. He disobeyed God by taking many wives and took matters into his own hands when he took a census of his army. And yet with all his shortcomings he was still "a man after God's own heart." David was a great sinner, but he was also very remorseful and repentant.[110] Within the lines of the psalms written by David we see a wide range of the human experience. When we realize that God cares for us and wants a genuine, intimate relationship with us we take the first step toward knowing God as David did.[111] As much as we love God we can still fall prey to our own human thoughts and emotions. It is in times such as those that we can turn to the book of Psalms for guidance and insight. Like David, we can prostrate ourselves before the Throne of Grace and cry, "Abba Father" knowing we serve a loving caring God who hears our prayers: *"And he said, Abba, Father, all things are possible unto thee; take away this cup from me: nevertheless not what I will, but what thou wilt"*. (Mark 14:36)

Next, we will look at the life of Moses, who although he wrote only one or two psalms, is perhaps one of the most beloved people in the Bible. Moses' story, filled with the frivolity of the human condition, draws us to him. Moses is the only other person in the Bible, besides Jesus, whose life is recorded from birth to death. We are given the opportunity to share in his experiences. We understand the anguish of a mother as she puts her baby in a small ark and sends it down stream to save him from the cruel edict of the King of Egypt. We rejoice with Moses' mother when through the hand of God, she is given her own child to wet-nurse from the daughter of Pharaoh, who drew him from the river. We watch and wait as Moses goes from the son of Pharaoh to the savior of his people, who after forty years in exile in Midian, has returned from the desert with the claim that he has been sent by the "I AM THAT I AM" to free them from three thousand years of bondage. And after an endless series of failed attempts to leave, due to Pharaoh's refusal to "Let my people go", we sit with baited breath awaiting the promised plagues that follow. This Moses, leading a downtrodden band of hopefuls to the promise land, is accredited with writing Psalm Ninety.

It is believed that Moses wrote the ninetieth Psalm during his time in the wilderness with the children of Israel. This would make it one of the oldest psalms. It is also the first psalm in the fourth division of the book of Psalms, which means it correlates with the book of Numbers in the Pentateuch. In this psalm Moses begins by declaring God to be their dwelling place: *"LORD, thou hast been our dwelling place in all generations"*. (Psalm 90:1)

The Israelites were going through the biggest transition of their lives. They left Egypt, which had been their home for more than three thousand years to head to the land of Canaan, a land filled with unknown obstacles. The heavens above and their earthly tents below were now the place they called home. Following a pillar of cloud by day and fire by night as their guide, Moses looks to God to be their only true dwelling place. According to the Strong's Exhaustive Concordance, the Hebrew word used in this verse is the word *"moan"* meaning dwelling place; help, habitation. Here we see Moses reminding God that the children of Israel know God as the divine source of refuge. God Himself had always been the dwelling place, the Tabernacle for the chosen people of God for all generations. Moses allows himself to reflect on his God. Everyone called by God finds a safe-haven, a refuge of protection. With more than 500 years between Moses and Abraham, Moses remembers that Abraham abided in God. Moses ponders, *"in all the generations"* and he sees Isaac, Jacob and Joseph safe in the master's arms, *"from everlasting to everlasting, thou art God"*; he is secure in the knowledge of the eternal God.

The modern-day Christian finds that same sense of security in Jesus. He is our tabernacle and through the power of the Holy Spirit, He dwells in us as we reside in Him. Paul says it best in his sermon on Mars' Hill, "*For in him, we live, and move, and have our being;*" (Acts 17:28a).

When we do not know where to begin or cannot find the right to words to say, we can rely upon the songs and the wisdom of those who have called upon God before us. Like a good cookbook the psalms are our partners in prayer. They reek of the meals of an accomplished chef whose experience and knowledge are reflected in the fine cuisine and notable ingredients.

CHAPTER 7

DESSERT

'Tis So Sweet

It doesn't matter if it's a family cookout, a baby shower or an elaborate celebration the meal just isn't complete until the dessert is served. It could be something as rich as New York Style Cheesecake or as simple as a demitasse of Jell-o with a swirl of whip crème topping, but a finale of some sort is required to complete the occasion. The meal itself has provided you with an ample serving, but you still desire a little delicacy to top it off.

There is a rare and beautiful unexpected gem in the lines of the melodic Old Testament Book of Psalms; the sweet gift of salvation. Here, between the preponderance of praise and the cries for help, you will find Jesus. The sweet-smelling savor of the Lord permeates your spirit and within the songs of the children of Israel you see the Messiah. We know that Jesus is not directly referenced and still we recognize Him. The King of Kings and Lord of Lords is ever present and yet to come. The revelation of our heavenly king resonates from the scriptures through the words of the psalmist:

> "O come, let us sing unto the Lord: let us make a joyful noise to the rock of our salvation.
> Let us come before his presence with thanksgiving, and make a joyful noise unto him with psalms.
> For the Lord is a great God, and a great King above all gods"
> (Psalm 95:1-2)

Jesus is the rock of our salvation and Lord of all. He makes Himself known to those who believe. He is the head of our lives:

> "The Lord reigneth, he is clothed with majesty; the Lord is clothed with strength, wherewith he hath girded himself: the world also is stablished, that it cannot be moved.
> Thy throne is established of old: thou art from everlasting" (Psalm 93:1-2)

He will return for those who have received him. He is eternal:

> "Before the Lord: for he cometh, for he cometh to judge the earth: he shall judge the world with righteousness, and the people with his truth" (Psalm 96:13).

Jesus represents the one and only unadulterated truth for the child of God. We are clothed in His righteousness:

"And I saw heaven open, and behold a white horse; and he that sat upon him was called Faithful and True, and in righteousness he doth judge and make war" (Revelation 19:11).

There are eleven Royal Psalms which speak directly to the reign of the earthly king, but many believe these psalms also make reference to our heavenly king. An additional seven psalms have a Messianic overtone which declare the Lord as King and address His attributes:

- The Lord God Reigns
- The Lord is King
- The Lord is Sovereign in Righteousness and Justice
- The Lord is Sovereign over the gods/idols
- The Lord is Sovereign in Creation
- The Lord is Sovereign in Eternity
- The Lord is Sovereign Over the Nations
- The Lord is Sovereign in His Choice/Care of Israel
- The Lord is Sovereign in Judgment
- The Lord is Sovereign in His Holiness
- The Lord is Sovereign Over the Future[112]

The 16th century theologian Martin Luther used Psalm 110 as the subject of his sermons developed in the spring of 1538. In this psalm he saw the entire Christian gospel:

This is the high and chief Psalm of our dear Lord Jesus Christ, in which His Person, and His resurrection,

> Ascension, and His whole kingdom are so clearly and powerfully set forth, that nothing of a similar kind can be found in all the writings of the Old Testament. It is therefore meet and right that it should always be sung and expounded at such festivals of our Lord as Easter, Ascension, and Whitsuntide.[113]

The power of the revelation of Christ in the psalms is the ability to recognize Him throughout the entire scope of the Old Testament. It is easy to hear the voice of Jesus in the New Testament as it speaks specifically to His life, ministry and resurrection. Many Bibles have the words of Jesus embossed in red letters. But when we can see Jesus between the lines of the Old Testament inside the hidden treasures of the symbolism we can move to new heights.

Within the melodious lines of the psalms not only do you find Jesus but also the sweet afterglow of the Holy Spirit. In the Old Testament the manifestation of the Holy Spirit was the physical representation of God to the children of Israel. They recognize God as omnipotent, omnipresent and omniscience yet invisible to the naked eye. However, in certain instances the Spirit of the Lord could be felt or seen. These occurrences are recorded throughout the scriptures: *"And Moses went out, and told the people the words of the LORD, and gathered the seventy men of the elders of the people, and set them around the tabernacle. And the LORD came down in a cloud, and spake unto him, and took of the spirit that was upon him, and gave it unto the seventy elders: and it came to pass, that, when the spirit rested upon them, they prophesied, and did not cease."* (Numbers 11:24-25) This is the same move of the Holy Spirit represented by the pillar of cloud and fire that lead the children of Israel through the wilderness and rested above the Ark of the Covenant when the tabernacle pattern was completed. "*So Moses finished the work. Then a cloud covered the tent of the congregation, and the glory of the LORD filled the tabernacle*". (Exodus 40:33b-34)

Many of the songs contained in the book of Psalms were used to minister to the Lord in the Tabernacle. The Sons of Korah during the time of King David became leaders in choral and orchestral music in the temple:[114] "*And these are they whom David set over the service of song in the house of the LORD, after that the ark had rest.*" (1 Chronicles 6:31) There are quite a few psalms, which have been attributed to these men. Many contain familiar verses:

> "*As the hart panteth after the water brooks, so panteth my soul after thee, o God*". (Psalm 41:1)
>
> "*Who is the King of glory? The LORD strong and mighty, the Lord mighty in battle*". (Psalm 24:8)
>
> "*Be still, and know that I am God: I will be exalt among the heathen, I will be exalted in the earth*". (Psalm 46:10)
>
> "*For a day in thy courts is better than a thousand. I had rather be a doorkeeper in the house of God, than to dwell in the tent of wickedness*". (Psalm 84:10)

These beautiful psalms express a spirit of gratitude and humility to an awesome mighty God.[115] There is no wonder we can sense the presence of the Holy Spirit radiating from them, for these are the songs sung in the wilderness as they marched behind the pillar of cloud, songs written by those who were chosen to minister continually to the Lord night and day.

New Testament Christians have the privilege of a personal relationship with God through the sacrifice of Jesus and the power of the Holy Spirit. The beauty of the Holy Spirit is His ability to reveal Jesus to us. We come to know Jesus for ourselves. He is our Savior and so we taste the sweet nectar of His presence daily in our lives. In his book, The Pursuit of God, A.W. Tozer states it thusly:

> They desire God above all. They are athirst to taste for themselves the "piercing sweetness" of the love of Christ above whom all the holy prophets did write and the psalmist did sing. (Tozer A. J., 1958)[116]

Godly women of the Middle Ages called Beguines formed Christian communities to pursue Christ and cultivate a personal relationship with the Lord. In their writings they describe their own encounters with God, often depicting their experience of God's love in terms of "sweetness".[117] Jesus Christ must be revealed by the Holy Spirit; no man knows the things of God but by the Holy Spirit: (Tozer A. , The Counselor; Straight Talk about the Holy Spirit. Revised Edition., 2009)[118] *"Now we have received, not the spirit of the world, but the spirit which is of God; that we might know the things that are freely given to us of God."* (1 Corinthians 2:12) God knows Himself, and the Holy Spirit knows God because the Holy Spirit is God, and no man can know God except by the Holy Spirit.[119]

Once we have experience Jesus in our lives we are never quite the same. The sweet fragrance of His love permeates our being.
The writer of this song says it best:

> 'Tis so sweet to trust in Jesus, Just to take Him at His word,
>
> Just to rest upon His promise, Just to know, "Thus saith the Lord."

Jesus, Jesus, how I trust Him! How I've proved Him o'er and o'er!
Jesus, Jesus, precious Jesus! O for grace to trust him more![120]

CHAPTER 8

THE RIDE HOME

The most wonderful thing about a good meal is that even when it's over the residual effects are long lasting. You cherish the experience. You have thoroughly enjoyed every aspect of each course. As you ride home your mind aimlessly wonders through the events of the evening. You turn to your spouse, ready for stimulating conversation, but all you can think about is the meal. Your thoughts are consumed by what you have just eaten. Your conversation reflects your thoughts. Which dish was your favorite? Will I visit this particular restaurant again? Can I duplicate the recipe at home? You have just dined at the Master's Table and there is an indescribable joy within your soul. You are filled with a peace that passes all understanding. You have tasted the Living Water and drank from the well that will never run dry. You will thirst no more. And all you want to do is share this incredible feeling with everyone you know. You want to tell anyone who is willing to listen, "I know a man and His name is Jesus".

When you begin to feast on the Word of God you are transformed. You become a new creature in Christ. Your perception of the world is altered and even in the midst of strife you find hope and peace. You no longer observe the world around you with mere earthly eyes for through God's Word; your spiritual senses have been awakened. We are to share our faith and tell nonbelievers about the wonderful changes Jesus Christ has made in our lives.[121]

You want others to receive the blessings of God. The lyrics from the song "Tell Somebody" by the William Brothers summarizes it best:

> You need to tell somebody, tell somebody about Jesus
> How He set you free, gave you the victory.
> Tell somebody, tell somebody about Jesus
> Tell somebody about the goodness of the Lord.

The Bible tells us that when Jesus ascended into heaven to return to the Father, He would send us His Spirit: "But ye shall receive power, after that the Holy Ghost is come upon you: and ye shall be witnesses unto me both in Jerusalem, and in all Judea, and in Samaria, and unto the utter most parts of the earth." (Acts 1:8) God has equipped us with the power and direction we need to be His disciples here on earth. Power and witness should be a trademark of all Christians.[122] It is His desire that we spread the good news about Jesus. We are endued with the Holy Spirit so that we can accomplish the will of the Father without hesitation everywhere we go. In Acts 1:8 He tells us to be His witnesses in three specific locations: Jerusalem, Judea and Samaria. Jerusalem is symbolic of our home, the place we consider our neighborhood or where we currently reside. The people we witness to would be those living in our household, our extended family and friends, as well as the people we come into contact on a regular basis. Every persons Jerusalem is different.[123] Judea represents the other communities or cities surrounding our regular encounters or the outskirts of our Jerusalem. Samaria would represent the cities or surrounding communities that are of a different culture or who are antagonistic towards each other and us. We know this because there was a bitter hatred between the Jews and the Samaritans, yet Jesus tells His witnesses to carry the message of salvation to their enemies.[124] This edict from Jesus gives us a wide range of options to fulfill our call of discipleship. We have an opportunity to share the gospel with our family, our co-workers, or strangers on the street. Because each of us has our own "Jerusalem," the parameters of our Judea and Samaria are very individualistic. For example, if the co-worker in the cubicle next to me is very antagonistic towards me and my beliefs, he could be my Samaria, or my unsaved family member who I see occasional on holidays could be my Judea. Jesus gave us a pattern of discipleship, not in any specific order or location, just the understanding that we have been given the spiritual boldness to witness Christ whenever and wherever we have the opportunity.

Our final destination for discipleship in Acts 1:8 is "*unto the utter most parts of the earth*". This constitutes the whole world. As Christians we are expected to spread the gospel to anyone who has not yet heard about Jesus. It is God's desire that everyone receive the gift of salvation: "*The Lord is not slack concerning his promise, as some men count slackness; but is longsuffering to us-ward, not willing that any should perish, but that all should come to repentance*". (1 Peter 3:9) Jesus tell us that the gospel must be preached before He returns: "*And this gospel of the kingdom shall be preached in all the world for a witness unto all nations; and then shall the end come*". (Matthew 24:14) Scriptures such as these should encourage us to support our mission fields both home and abroad. We understand that we are not physically able to be or go everywhere but at the same time we want to make sure God's Word is shared throughout the world. It is our goal that everyone can feast on the Word of God and receive the gift of salvation.

In Matthew 28:19-20, The Great Commission, Jesus gives us instructions for our mission. We are to baptize believers in the name of the Trinity. We must teach all nations to observe the commandments given in God's Word. And we do not attempt to accomplish this alone because He is always with us: "*Go ye therefore, and teach all nations, baptizing them in the name of the Father, and of the Son, and of the Holy Ghost: Teaching them to observe all things whatsoever I have commanded you: and, lo, I am with you always, even unto the end of the world.*" (Matthew 28:19-20) For some the Great Commission is considered an insurmountable task that can only be accomplished by those who are called to the ministry with very specific roles as mentioned in the five-fold ministry of Ephesians: "*And he gave some, apostles; and some, prophets; and some evangelist; and some, pastors and teachers; For the perfecting of the saints, for the work of the ministry, for the edifying of the body of Christ*". (Ephesian 4:11-12) While we know that God calls individuals to certain ministries we must also be cognizant that every believer has the ability to do the work of the Lord through the power of the Holy Spirit. For this reason, prayer is such a vial part of our Christian walk and our ability to accomplish God's will.

Prayer is a two-way fellowship and communication with God. (King, Experiencing God; How to Live the Full Adventure of Knowing and Doing the Will of God, 1988)[125] We need to pray so that we can hear from God and know what He wants us to do. God will speak to us in a variety of ways. He will use the Holy Spirit, the Word of God or the people of God. Often when we pray God will lay scriptures on our heart to validate His communication with you. When the Holy Spirit reveals a spiritual truth to you in prayer, He is present and working actively in your life.[126] What happens as you seek God's will in prayer? The sequence is this:

1. God takes initiative by causing you to want to pray.
2. The Holy Spirit, through the Word of God, reveals to you the will of God.
3. In the Spirit, you pray in agreement with the will of God.
4. You adjust your life to the truth (to God).
5. You look and listen for confirmation or further direction from the Bible, circumstances, and the church (other believers).
6. You obey.
7. God works in you and through you to accomplish His purposes.
8. You experience Him just as the Spirit revealed as you prayed.[127]

When we pray, surrendering our will to God and looking to Him for the answers, discipleship becomes an effortless task. You will still be met with resistance but the Spirit that is working through you is the same Spirit that will move on the heart of the listener. Salvation is the work of the Holy Spirit. It is your job to witness to His power and presence in your life.

So, the meal has come to an end but everything about it still lingers in your spirit. It was the best time you ever had. You invite others to dine at His table: "Come and drink from the well that will never run dry and you shall never thirst again. Taste the Bread of Life and you will never know another hunger day. This is the meal, which last from every lasting till every lasting. And don't worry about the cost because Jesus paid it all."

CONCLUSION

This journey into the book of Psalms has been a mere glimpse of the magnitude and depth of God's Word. The Bible is the inspired word of God. It gives us insight into the will of God. It demonstrates the intensity of His love. It reveals the complexity of His character. The Bible allows us to come into the full knowledge of God for ourselves because it is a living word.

As children of the Most High God, we know that we are created in His image. We were fashioned from the dust of the earth and then God breathed the breath of life into us. We are told in Genesis 2:7 that: "*the LORD God formed man of the dust of the ground, and breathed into his nostrils the breath of life; and man became a living soul* [*nephesh*]." The word "soul" comes from the Hebrew term *nephesh*, which means "life", "life force", "soul", and "the seat of emotion and desire". When God gathered dust out of the ground and shaped it into human form, man was merely a lump of clay. But when He breathed into his nostrils, the first man received life from God. God is a Spirit being. Therefore, we know that it is our spirit that is liken to God's image while our body reflects His earthly design. We, as created beings, are a reflection of God.[128]

Our physical body requires nourishment on a regular basis to survive. Likewise, our spirit must be feed if it is to thrive. To have a healthy body it is suggested that we eat three well-balanced meals a day, exercise on a regular basis and get plenty of rest. Our spirit also requires a regular regimen. Nourishment of the spirit can be accomplished in a variety of ways but interaction with the Heavenly Father is the key to a healthy soul. The spirit needs prayer, meditation and God's Word for basic maintenance. We must spend time with God's Word, so we can gain a better understanding of His character, wisdom, and desire for our lives.

Prayer is the vehicle through which we begin to communicate with God. We must converse with God to recognize His voice. God primarily speaks by the Holy Spirit through the Bible, prayer, circumstances, and church.[129] He wants us to know and recognize his voice to cultivate a personal relationship with us. Coming into the knowledge of God is an essential function of the Holy Spirit: *"Even the Spirit of truth; whom the world cannot receive, because it seeth him not, neither knoweth him: but ye know him; for he dwelleth with you and shall be in you"*. (John 14:17)

In addition to prayer, we must read, study and meditate upon the Word of God. The Bible describes God's complete revelation of Himself to humanity.[130] Our ability to hear God speak and fully understand the revelation of His spiritual truths is a product of time spent in the Word. We plot a pre-destined course to our Savior, reading the scriptures with a sense of anticipation. We close our eyes and let the Word ruminate in our spirit awaiting the sound of His voice. God is in the words because the Word is God. Understanding spiritual truths does not lead you to an encounter with God; it is the encounter with God.[131] As we study the

Word of God the Holy Spirit begins to open our understanding about God and His purpose and His ways: "*Study to shew thyself approved unto God, a workman that needeth not to be ashamed, rightly dividing the word of truth.*" (2 Timothy 2:15)

The book of Psalms is the hymnbook of the Bible. Within these hymns are generations of prayers reflecting the hopes, dreams, trials and tribulations of God's chosen people. The psalms are vital to our spiritual growth because they speak to the human condition and reflect a deep desire to commune with God. I believe therefore God inspired me to write about the book of Psalms as it pertains to our complete spiritual health and overall well-being in the kingdom. The Psalms are spiritual nourishment.

David, the most popular author of numerous psalms, understood the value of spiritual nutrition through his relationship with God. He made God his closest confidant and most trusted ally. David knew the potential inherent in a covenant relationship, and he trusted God more than anyone else.[132] God was the desire of his heart. Psalm Sixty-Three epitomizes the sum total of his hunger and thirst for God.

> "*O God, thou art my God; early will I seek thee: my soul thirsteth for thee, my flesh longeth for thee in a dry and thirsty land, where no water is; To see thy power and thy glory, so as I have seen in the sanctuary. Because thy lovingkindness is better than life, my lips shall praise thee. Thus will I bless thee while I live: I will lift up my hands in they name. My soul shall be satisfied as with marrow and fatness; and my mouth shall praise thee with joyful lips: When I remember thee on my bed, and meditate on thee in the night watches. Because thou hast*

been my help, therefore in the shadow of thy wings will I rejoice. My soul followeth hard after thee: thy right hand upholdeth me." (Psalm 63:1-8)

David wrote this psalm whilst in the wilderness of Judah. He was separated from the Temple, the dwelling place of God, and his soul longs for his friend. He does not allow the physical distance between them to squelch his worship. He begins to sing, *"O God, thou art my God; early will I seek thee."* (Psalm 63:1a) He knows the dwelling place of Jehovah is larger than any Temple. As a young shepherd boy, he saw God in the beauty all around him. David saw that the master of the universe had spared nothing when it came to His creation.[133] God's handiwork moved David's heart; *"my soul thirsteth for thee, my flesh longeth for thee in a dry and thirsty land, where no water is"*. (Psalm 63:1b) David is not concerned with the lack of physical water. He is in a spiritual drought, a dry place where he needs God, who is the keeper of his soul, to quench his spiritual thirst. He longs for the same power and glory he has experienced in the sanctuary to be ever present with him now. In verses three and four, David shifts to a position of praise, glorifying God with the praises of his lips. With his hands lifted upward towards heaven, he proceeds to bless the name of the Lord. By verse five, David discerns that the satisfaction of his soul rest with spiritual fulfillment. He is consumed with moments of joy and thanksgiving. He pauses to ponder the greatness of his God: *"When I remember thee upon my bed, and meditate on thee in the night watches"*. (Psalm 63:6) Throughout verses seven and eight, He is reminded of the God who has been both his divine helper and constant protector. It is God who hides him beneath His wings. The God who made heaven and earth, the Creator, supports him in His all-powerful right hand. David makes this profound statement: *"My soul followeth hard after thee."* (Psalm 63:8a) This verse echoes the sentiments of the spirit, longing for the soul quenching presence of God.

A daily dose of the gospel becomes not only our soul's nourishment but also becomes our substance. Here in these beloved songs of the Bible you can find the soul satisfying Spirit of the Lord. It is my prayer, that as you hunger and thirst for the righteousness of God, you will make the Book of Psalms an integral part of your soul's spiritual healthy diet.

Endnotes

[1] Lehman Strauss, **Man A Trinity (Spirit, Soul, Body)**, from the series: Death & Afterword Chapter 2. www.bible.org (Accessed February 12, 2014)

[2] All Scripture quotations are taken from the **King James Bible** version unless otherwise noted, Thompson Chain Reference, Fourth Improved Edition, 1964.

[3] David J. Stewart, "**Understanding The Human Soul**", (December 2012). www.jesus-is-savior.com. (Accessed January 31, 2015)

[4] Watchman Nee, **Collected Works of Watchman Lee, Set 1 Vol. 13: The Spiritual Man (2)** Chapter 1. www.worldinvisible.com. (Accessed January 31, 2015)

[5] www.holiness-preaching.org/songlyrics

[6] N.T. Wright, **The Case For The Psalms: Why They Are Essential**. (New York, N.Y.: HarperCollins Publishers, 2013), 2.

[7] C. Hassell Bullock, **Encountering The Book Of Psalms; A Literary and Theological Introduction**. (Grand Rapids, Michigan: Baker Academic, 2001), 22.

[8] Five Books of Psalms, www.lwbc.co.uk. (Accessed February 22, 2014)

[9] Information obtained from Dr. William R. Glaze, Pastor, Bethany Baptist Church, (Pittsburgh, PA), Sermon series on the Book of Psalms.

[10] C. Hassell Bullock, **Encountering The Book Of Psalms; A Literary and Theological Introduction**. (Grand Rapids, Michigan: Baker Academic, 2001), 58.

[11] The Psalms of David, www.ifcj.org. (Accessed March 31, 2015).

[12] Ibid, 36.

[13] Merrill F. Unger, "**The Nature of Hebrew Poetry**," *Journal; Bibliotheca Sacra*, Vol. BSCA 108:431 (July 1951). www.galaxie.com. (Accessed March 29, 2015), 282.

[14] C. Hassell Bullock, **Encountering The Book Of Psalms; A Literary and Theological Introduction.** (Grand Rapids, Michigan: Baker Academic, 2001), 39.

[15] Merrill F. Unger, "**The Nature of Hebrew Poetry,**" *Journal; Bibliotheca Sacra*, Vol. BSCA 108:431 (July 1951). www.galaxie.com. (Accessed March 29, 2015).

[16] C. Hassell Bullock, **Encountering The Book Of Psalms; A Literary and Theological Introduction.** (Grand Rapids, Michigan: Baker Academic, 2001), 41.

[17] Ibid, 41.

[18] Ibid, 43.

[19] **The New Open Bible**, Study Edition, Nashville: Thomas Nelson, 1990, 630.

[20] Ibid, 634.

[21] N.T. Wright, **The Case For The Psalms: Why They Are Essential.** (New York, N.Y.: HarperCollins Publishers, 2013), 22.

[22] Ibid, 23.

[23] Bethany House, **The Prayers of David: Becoming A Person after God's Own Heart** (Bloomington, MN: Bethany House Publishers, 2007), 129.

[24] Charles H. Spurgeon, The Treasury of David: Exposition, www.spurgeon.org. (Accessed March 9, 2015)

[25] Ibid.

[26] Ibid.

[27] Bethany House, **The Prayers of David: Becoming A Person after God's Own Heart** (Bloomington, MN: Bethany House Publishers, 2007), 129.

[28] Thomas Merton, **Praying The Psalms**, (Collegeville, MN: The Liturgical Press, 1956), 13.

[29] Walter Brueggemann, **Praying The Psalms: Engaging Scripture and the Life of the Spirit**, (Eugene, OR: Cascade Books, 2007), 30.

[30] William R. Glaze, **Prayer Facilitator's Training Manual**, (Pittsburgh, PA), 24.

[31] Walter Brueggemann, **Praying The Psalms: Engaging Scripture and the Life of the Spirit**, (Eugene, OR: Cascade Books, 2007), 46.

[32] Thomas Merton, **Praying The Psalms**, (Collegeville, MN: The Liturgical Press, 1956), 11.

[33] Ibid, 46.

[34] Clift & Kathleen Richards, **Praying the Psalms**, (Tulsa, OK: Victory House, Inc., 2003), 21.

[35] Ibid, 19.

[36] Psalms of Degrees Psalms 120-134 are also known as "songs of ascent." These are psalms that were sung by the Israelites on their annual journey to Jerusalem to celebrate the feasts at the Temple. From Sermon by Dr. William R. Glaze, "GOD will not NOD on the JOB". Bethany Baptist Church, Pittsburgh, PA (November 14, 2004).

[37] Clift & Kathleen Richards, **Praying the Psalms**, (Tulsa, OK: Victory House, Inc., 2003), 16.

[38] Ibid, 111.

[39] Ibid, 115.

[40] N.T. Wright, **The Case For The Psalms: Why They Are Essential**. (New York, N.Y.: HarperCollins Publishers, 2013), 167.

[41] Thomas Merton, **Praying The Psalms**, (Collegeville, MN: The Liturgical Press, 1956), 24.

[42] Clift & Kathleen Richards, **Praying the Psalms**, (Tulsa, OK: Victory House, Inc., 2003), 17.

[43] Ibid, 17.

[44] **Psalm 23 (The Lord is My Shepherd)**, www.shmoop.com. (Accessed March 22, 2014)

[45] Ibid.

[46] **Psalm 23**, www.jewishpub.org. (Accessed March 23, 2015)

[47] Ibid.

[48] Walter Brueggemann, **Spirituality of the Psalms**. (Minneapolis: Fortress, 2002), 18.

[49] **Psalm 23 (The Lord is My Shepherd)**, www.shoop.com. (Accessed March 22, 2014)

[50] **Psalm 23 (The Lord is My Shepherd)**, www.shmoop.com. (Accessed March 22, 2014)

[51] Karl Jacobson, " **Through the Pistol Smoke Dimly: Psalm 23 in Contemporary Film and Song**," *SBL Forum,* n.p. [Cited Jan 2009]. Online:http://sbl-site.org/Article.aspx?ArticleID=796 (Accessed March 22, 2014)

[52] Ibid.

[53] Robert J. Morgan, **The Lord Is My Shepherd**. (New York, NY: Howard Books, 2013), 7

[54] Bethany House, **The Prayers of David: Becoming A Person after God's Own Heart.** (Bloomington, MN: Bethany House Publishers, 2007), 14.

[55] Robert J. Morgan, **The Lord Is My Shepherd**. (New York, NY: Howard Books, 2013), 21.

[56] Ibid, 9.

[57] **Psalm 23**, www.jewishpub.org. (Accessed March 23, 2015)

[58] What is Anointing? What does it mean to be Anointed? www.gotquestions.org. (Accessed March 4, 2015)

[59] Ibid.

[60] Ibid.

[61] Robert J. Morgan, **The Lord Is My Shepherd**. (New York, NY: Howard Books, 2013), 169.

[62] Robert J. Morgan, **The Lord Is My Shepherd**. (New York, NY: Howard Books, 2013), xiii

[63] Areon Potter, **Psalm 91 The Dweller**. (Mustang, OK: Tate Publishing & Enterprises, LLC, 2009), 21.

[64] Ibid, 21.

[65] Ibid, 27-28.

[66] Ibid, 47.

[67] Charles Caldwell Ryrie, The Ryrie Study Bible. (Chicago: Moody Press, 1978).

[68] Areon Potter, **Psalm 91 The Dweller**. (Mustang, OK: Tate Publishing & Enterprises, LLC, 2009), 48.

[69] Ibid, 48-49.

[70] Ibid, 77.

[71] Ibid, 77.

[72] Ibid, 29.

[73] Ibid, 37.

[74] Ibid, 39.

[75] Ibid, 65 & 69.

[76] Ibid, 75-76.

[77] Ibid, 78.

[78] Ibid, 73.

[79] Ibid, 73.

[80] Ibid, 20.

[81] Ibid, 74.

[82] Ibid, 20.

[83] The Answer To Trust; Psalm 91:14 MacLaren's Expositions. www.biblehub.com. (Accessed January 31, 2015)

[84] Areon Potter, **Psalm 91 The Dweller**. (Mustang, OK: Tate Publishing & Enterprises, LLC, 2009), 229.

[85] New American Standard Bible; **The Open Bible** (Nashville, TN: Thomas Nelson Publishers, 1979)

[86] Steve J. Cole, Psalm 150: The Priority Of Praise. www.bible.org. (Accessed March 27, 2015)

[87] Steve J. Cole, Psalm 150: The Priority Of Praise. www.bible.org. (Accessed March 27, 20015)

[88] Ibid.

[89] Ibid.

[90] Ibid.

[91] Ibid.

[92] Hebrew Words for Praise, www.buddysheets.tripod.com. (Accessed March 27, 2015).

[93] Elements of a Gourmet Meal, www.etiquettescholar.com. (Accessed January 15, 2015).

[94] N.T. Wright, **The Case For The Psalms: Why They Are Essential**. (New York, N.Y.: HarperCollins Publishers, 2013), 164.

[95] M. Basil Pennington, **Psalms: A Spiritual Commentary**, (Woodstock, VT: SkyLight Paths Publishing, 2008), 58.

[96] William R. Glaze, Intimacy and Thirsting for God, Taken from his commentary on Psalms 42 (Bethany Baptist Church, Pittsburgh, PA) March 31, 2015 via email.

[97] Thomas Merton, **Praying The Psalms**, (Collegeville, MN: The Liturgical Press, 1956), 7.

[98] Book Of Psalms, www.gotquestions.org. (Accessed March 31, 20015).

[99] Jeffrey Kranz, "**Who Wrote the Psalms? Hint: it wasn't just David**". www.overviewbible.com. From The Overview Bible Project, April 24, 2014, (Accessed March 31, 2015).

[100] Charles R. Swindoll, **Psalms,** The Bible – Teaching Ministry of Charles R. Swindoll. www.insight,org, (Accessed June 1, 2014).

[101] Jack Zavada, King David, A Man After God's Heart, www.christianity.about.com. (Accessed March 31, 2015).

[102] Jeffrey Kranz, "**Who Wrote the Psalms? Hint: it wasn't just David**". www.overviewbible.com. From The Overview Bible Project, April 24, 2014, (Accessed March 31, 2015).

[103] The Psalms of David, www.ifcj.org. (Accessed March 31, 2015).

[104] Ibid.

[105] Ibid.

[106] Bethany House, **The Prayers of David: Becoming A Person after God's Own Heart** (Bloomington, MN: Bethany House Publishers, 2007), 30.

[107] Ibid, 31.

[108] The Psalms of David, www.ifcj.org. (Accessed March 31, 2015).

[109] Jack Zavada, King David, A Man After God's Heart, www.christianity.about.com. (Accessed March 31, 2015)

[110] Ibid.

[111] Bethany House, **The Prayers of David: Becoming A Person after God's Own Heart** (Bloomington, MN: Bethany House Publishers, 2007), 22.

[112] C. Hassell Bullock, **Encountering The Book Of Psalms; A Literary and Theological Introduction**. (Grand Rapids, Michigan: Baker Academic, 2001), 195.

[113] Quoted by Jane T. Stoddart, **The Psalms for Every Day**, (London: Hodder and Stoughton, 1939), 267.

[114] Who were the Sons of Korah in the Old Testament, www.gotquestions.org. (Accessed March 31, 20015).

[115] Ibid.

[116] A.W. Tozer, The Pursuit of God (Harrisburg, PA, 1958) Kindle Loc.

[117] Glen E. Myers, The Sweet Presence of Jesus, www.cbn.com. (Accessed April 2, 2015)

[118] A.W. Tozer, The Counselor; Straight Talk about the Holy Spirit, Revised Edition (Camp Hill, PA, Wing Spread Publishers, 2009) Kindle Loc. 343

[119] Ibid, Loc. 249

[120] **The New National Baptist Hymnal**, (Nashville, Tenn.: National Baptist Publishing Board, 1997), 196.

[121] Discipleship, www.gotquestions.org. (Accessed March 31, 20015).

[122] Have We Forgotten Jerusalem? Acts 1:8, www.step-by-step.org. (Accessed April 2, 2015).

[123] Ibid.

[124] Ibid.

[125] Henry T. Blackaby & Claude V. King, **Experiencing God; How to Live the Full Adventure of Knowing and Doing the Will of God**, (Nashville, TN: Broadman & Holman Publishers, 1998) 174.

[126] Ibid, 174.

[127] Ibid, 175.

[128] Bethany House, **The Prayers of David: Becoming A Person after God's Own Heart** (Bloomington, MN: Bethany House Publishers, 2007), 126.

[129] Henry T. Blackaby & Claude V. King, **Experiencing God: How to Live the Full Adventure of Knowing and Doing the Will of God**, (Nashville, TN: Broadman & Holman Publishers, 1998) 163.

[130] Ibid, 164.

[131] Ibid, 165.

[132] Bethany House, **The Prayers of David: Becoming A Person after God's Own Heart** (Bloomington, MN: Bethany House Publishers, 2007), 68.

[133] Ibid, 125.

Bibliography

Ayayo, H. A. (2007). *Hermeneutics; Principles and Process of Biblical Interpretation* (2nd Edition ed.). Grand Rapids, Michigan: Baker Academics.

Bethany House. (2007). *The Prayers of David: Becoming A Person After God's Own Heart.* Bloomington, MN, USA: Bethany House Publishers.

Bethany House. (2007). *The Prayers of David: Becoming A Person After God's Own Heart.* Bloomington, MN: Bethany House Publishers.

Bible Hub. (2004, January 1). *Bible Hub Online Bible Suite.* Retrieved January 31, 2015, from www.biblehub.com: http://biblehub.com/commentaries/

Bible Questions Answered. (2001, January 1). *Got Questions?* Retrieved March 4, 2015, from www.gotquestions.org: http://www.gotquestions.org

Bible Study Tools. (2014, January 1). *Bible Study Tools.* Retrieved March 27, 2015, from www.biblestudytools.com: http://www.biblestudytools.com/commentaries/

Bonhoeffer, D. (1974). *Psalms; The Prayer Book of the Bible.* Minneapolis, MN: Augsburg Fortress.

Brueggemann, W. (2007). *Praying The Psalms: Engaging Scripture and the Life of the Spirit.* Eugene, OR: Cascade Books.

Brueggemann, W. (2007). *Praying The Psalms: Engaging Scripture and the Life of the Spirit. Eugene.* Eugene, OR: Cascade Books.

Bullock, C. H. (2001). *Encountering The Book Of Psalms; A Literary and Theological Introduction.* Grand Rapids, Michigan: Baker Academic.

Bullock, C. H. (2001). *Encountering The Book Of Psalms; A Literary and Theological Introduction.* Grand Rapids, Michigan: Baker Academic.

Chan, F. (2008). *Crazy Love; Overwhelmed by a Relentless God.* Colorado Springs, Colorado: David C. Cook.

Cocherell, B. (2008, February 1). *The Process of Salvation.* Retrieved February 2, 2014, from www.bibleresearch.org: http://www.bibleresearch.org/gospelbook1/b1w8.html

Cole, S. J. (1993, January 1). *Bible.org.* Retrieved March 27, 2015, from www.bible.org: https://bible.org/seriespage/psalm-150-priority-praise

Etiquette Scholar. (2014, January 1). *Etiquette Scholar.* Retrieved January 15, 2015, from www.etiquettescholar.com: http://www.etiquettescholar.com/etiquette_scholar/dining_etiquette.html

Five Books of Psalms. (1995, January 1). Retrieved February 22, 2014, from www.lwbc.co.uk: http://www.lwbc.co.uk/5_books_of_psalms.htm

Gorman, M. J. (2009). *Elements of Biblical Exegesis* (Revised and Expanded Edition ed.). Grand Rapids, Michigan: Baker Academic.

Gospel Song Lyrics. (2007, January 1). Retrieved Feburary 1, 2014, from www.holiness-preaching.org/songlyrics: http://www.holiness-preaching.org/frame-SongLyrics.html

Hilber, J. W. (2013). *Psalms.* Grand Rapids, Michigan: Zondervan.

Hildebrand, L. (2012). *Prayers That Change Things.* Alachua, Florida: Bridge Logos Foundation.

International Fellowship of Christians and Jews. (1998, February 1). *International Fellowship of Christians and Jews.* Retrieved March 31, 2015, from www.ifcj.org: http://www.ifcj.org/site/DocServer/FCH302_DAVID_LESSON_1.pdf?docID=5785

Jacobson, K. (2009, January 1). *SBL Forum, n.p.* Retrieved March 22, 2014, from www.sbl-site.org: http://sbl-site.org//Articleaspx?ArticleID=796

King, H. T. (1988). *Experiencing God; How to Live the Full Adventure of Knowing and Doing the Will of God.* Nashville, Tennessee: Broadman & Holman Publishers.

King, H. T. (1998). *Experiencing God; How to Live the Full Adventure of Knowing and Doing the Will of God.* Nashville, Tennessee: Broadman & Holman Publishers.

Kranz, J. (2014, April 24). *The Overview Bible Project.* Retrieved March 31, 2015, from www.overviewbible.com: http://overviewbible.com/?s=Who+wrote+the+psalms%3F+hint+it+wasn%27t+David

Lee, W. (1996, August 1). *The Spiritual Man.* Retrieved January 31, 2015, from www.worldinvisible.com: http://www.worldinvisible.com/library/nee/sprtmnv1/1968v1c1.htm

Lewis, C. (2012). *Reflections on the Psalms.* New York, NY: Houghton Mifflin Harcourt Publishing Company.

Merton, T. (1956). *Praying The Psalms.* Collegeville, MN: The Liturgical Press, 1956.

Merton, T. (1956). *Praying The Psalms.* Collegeville, MN: The Liturgical Press.

Morgan, R. J. (2013). *The Lord Is My Shepherd.* New York, NY: Howrd Books.

Morgan, R. J. (2013). *The Lord Is My Shepherd.* New York, NY, USA: Howrd Books.

Myers, G. E. (2009, January 1). *The Sweet Presence of Jesus: Spiritual Life in God.* Retrieved April 2, 2015, from www.cbn.com: http://www.cbn.com/spirituallife/churchandministry/churchhistory/Myers_Beguines_Jesus_Sweet_Presence.aspx

Pennington, M. B. (2008). *Psalms: A Spiritual Commentary.* Woodstock, VT: SkyLight Paths Publishing.

Pennington, M. B. (2008). *Psalms: A Spiritual Commentary.* Woodstock, VT: SkyLight Paths Publishing.

Pierce, T. M. (2008). *Enthroned On Our Praise; An Old Testament Theology of Worship.* Nashville, TN: B & H Publishing Group.

Potter, A. (2009). *Psalms 91 The Dweller.* Mustang, OK: Tate Publishing & Enterprises, LLC.

Potter, A. (2009). *Psalms 91 The Dweller.* Mustang, OK: Tate Publishing & Enterprises, LLC,.

Richards, C. &. (2003). *Praying the Psalms*. Tulsa, OK, USA: Victory House, Inc.

Richards, C. &. (2003). *Praying the Psalms*. Tulsa, OK: Victory House, Inc.

Ruth, P. J. (2002). *Psalms 91; God's Umbrella of Protection*. Sisters, OR: The 1687 Foundation.

Shmoop Editorial Team. (2008, November 11). *Psalm 23 ("The Lord Is my Shepherd")*. Retrieved March 22, 2014, from www.shmoop.com: http://www.shmoop.com/psalm-23/

Spurgeon, C. H. (1995). *Prayer*. New Kensington, Pennsylvania: Whitaker House.

Step By Step World Outreach Ministries. (2007, May 1). *Step by Step World Ministries*. Retrieved April 2, 2015, from www.step-by-step.org: http://www.step-by-step.org/acts1-8.htm

Stewart, D. J. (2012, December 1). *jesus-is-savior*. Retrieved January 31, 2015, from www.jesus-is-savior: http://www.jesus-is-savior.com/Believer's%20Corner/Doctrines/spirit_soul_body.htm

Stewart, D. J. (2012, December 1). *Understanding The Human Soul*. Retrieved January 31, 2015, from www.jesus-is-savior.com: http://www.jesus-is-savior.com/Believer's%20Corner/Doctrines/spirit_soul_body.htm

Stewart, D. J. (December 1, 2012). *"Understanding The Human Soul."*. www.jesus-is-savior.com http://www.jesus-is-savior.com/Believer's%20Corner/Doctrines/spirit_soul_body.htm (accessed January 31, 2015).

Stoddart, J. T. (1939). *The Psalms for Every Day*. London: Hodder and Stoughton.

Strauss, L. (2004, June 14). *2. Man A Trinity (Spirit, Soul, Body) | Bible.org*. Retrieved February 12, 2014, from Bible.Org | Where the World Comes to Study the Bible: https://bible.org/seriespage/2-man-trinity-spirit-soul-body

Strauss, L. (June 14, 2004). *"2. Man A Trinity (Spirit, Soul, Body) | Bible.org."*. Bible.Org | Where the World Comes to Study the Bible https://bible.org/seriespage/2-man-trinity-spirit-soul-body

Suprgeon, C. H. (1885, January 1). *The Spurgeon Archives*. Retrieved March 9, 2015, from www.spurgeon.com: http://www.spurgeon.org/treasury/treasury.htm

Swindoll, C. R. (2009, June 1). *Book Of Psalms - Insight for Living Ministries*. Retrieved June 1, 2014, from www.insight.org: http://www.insight.org/resources/bible/psalms.html

The Jewish Publication Society. (2011, February 18). Retrieved March 23, 2015, from www.jewishpub.org: http://www.jewishpub.org/pdf/psalm23.pdf

Tozer, A. (1958). *The Pursuit of God*. Harrisburg, Pennsylvania: Christian Publications Inc.

Tozer, A. (2009). *The Counselor; Straight Talk about the Holy Spirit* (Revised Edition ed.). Camp Hill, Pennsylvania: Wing Spread Publishers.

Tozer, A. (2009). *The Counselor; Straight Talk about the Holy Spirit. Revised Edition*. Camp Hill, Pennsylvania: Wing Spread Publishers.

Tozer, A. J. (1958). *The Pursuit of God*. Harrisburg, Pennsylvani: Christian Publications, Inc.

Tripod. (2014, January 1). *Hebrew Words for Praise*. Retrieved March 27, 2015, from www.buddysheets.tripod.com: http://buddysheets.tripod.com/hebrewwordsforpraise.htm

Unger, M. F. (1951, July 1). *Galaxie Software Electronic Publishing*. Retrieved March 31, 2015, from www.galaxie.com: http://www.galaxie.com/article/bsac108-431-04

Wright, N. T. (2013). *The Case For The Psalms: Why They Are Essential*. New York, N.Y: HarperCollins Publishers.

Wright, N. T. (2013). *The Case For The Psalms: Why They Are Essential*. New York, N.Y.: HarperCollins Publishers.

Zavada, J. (2015, January 1). *King David - A Man After God's Own Heart*. Retrieved March 31, 2015, from www.christianity.about.com: http://christianity.about.com/od/oldtestamentpeople/a/King-David.htm

FURTHER READING

Ayayo, Henry A. Virkler & Karelynne Gerber. *Hermeneutics; Principles and Process of Biblical Interpretation.* 2nd Edition. Grand Rapids, Michigan: Baker Academics, 2007.

Bonhoeffer, Dietrich. *Psalms; The Prayer Book of the Bible.* Minneapolis, MN: Augsburg Fortress, 1974.

Chan, Francis. *Crazy Love; Overwhelmed by a Relentless God.* Colorado Springs, Colorado: David C. Cook, 2008.

Gorman, Michael J. *Elements of Biblical Exegesis.* Revised and Expanded Edition. Grand Rapids , Michigan: Baker Academic, 2009.

Hilber, John W. *Psalms.* Grand Rapids, Michigan: Zondervan, 2013.

Lewis, C.S. *Reflections on the Psalms.* New York, NY: Houghton Mifflin Harcourt Publishing Company, 2012.

Ruth, Peggy Joyce. *Psalms 91; God's Umbrella of Protection.* Sisters, OR: The 1687 Foundation, 2002.

Spurgeon, C. H. *Prayer.* New Kensington, Pennsylvania: Whitaker House, 1995.

Made in the USA
Columbia, SC
10 April 2024